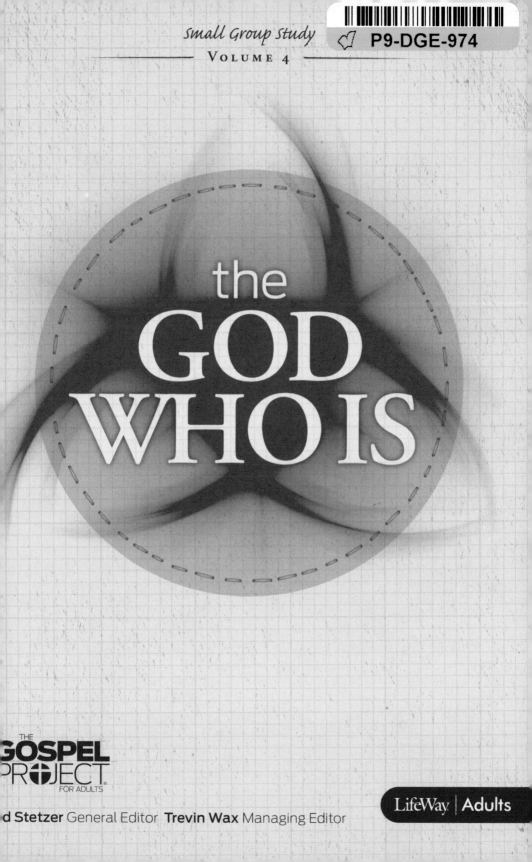

small Group Study

VOLUME 4

P9-DGE-974

the
GOD
WHO IS

THE
GOSPEL
PROJECT.
FOR ADULTS

LifeWay | Adults

d Stetzer General Editor Trevin Wax Managing Editor

© 2013 LifeWay Press®

No part of this work may be reproduced or transmitted in any form or by any means, electronic or mechanical, including photocopying and recording, or by any information storage or retrieval system, except as my be expressly permitted in writing by the publisher. Requests for permission should be addressed in writing to LifeWay Press®, One LifeWay Plaza, Nashville, TN 37234-0102.

ISBN: 978-1-4300-2537-5
Item: 005585510

Dewey Decimal Classification Number: 220.07
Subject Heading: BIBLE—STUDY \ THEOLOGY—STUDY \ GOSPEL—STUDY

We believe that the Bible has God for its author; salvation for its end; and truth, without any mixture of error, for its matter and that all Scripture is totally true and trustworthy. To review LifeWay's doctrinal guideline, please visit *www.lifeway.com/doctrinalguideline*.

Unless otherwise noted, all Scripture quotations are taken from the Holman Christian Standard Bible®, copyright 1999, 2000, 2002, 2003, 2009 by Holman Bible Publishers. Used by permission.

To order additional copies of this resource, write to LifeWay Church Resources; One LifeWay Plaza; Nashville, TN 37234-0113; phone toll free (800) 458-2772; fax (615) 251-5933; email *orderentry@lifeway.com*; order online at *www.lifeway.com*; or visit the LifeWay Christian Store serving you.

Printed in the United States of America.

Adult Ministry Publishing
LifeWay Church Resources
One LifeWay Plaza
Nashville, Tennessee 37234

Table of Contents

Writers

Part 1: God the Father

Kendell Easley is a professor of biblical studies at Union University in Jackson, Tennessee, and is the director of the Master of Christian Studies and Doctor of Ministry programs for Union's Stephen Olford Center. He has written ongoing curriculum for more than 20 years. Kendell is married to Nancy, and they have one married young adult son.

Part 2: God the Son

Geoff Ashley, who also wrote chapter 1, is the Discipleship Resource Pastor for The Village Church in Flower Mound, Texas. He received a ThM from Dallas Theological Seminary in 2009 and has been on staff at The Village since 2006, overseeing the development of theological resources.

Part 3: God the Spirit

Lizette Beard has earned degrees in Religious Studies (University of Missouri) and Missiology (The Southern Baptist Theological Seminary) and is pursuing a PhD in applied theology (North American Church Planting) at Southeastern Baptist Theological Seminary. She worked for the International Mission Board in Abidjan, Cote d'Ivoire (West Africa) and now serves as a project manager for LifeWay Research.

The Gospel Project

Introduction

Some people see the Bible as a collection of stories with morals for life application. But it is so much more. Sure, the Bible has some stories in it, but it is also full of poetry, history, codes of law and civilization, songs, prophecy, letters—even a love letter. When you tie it all together, something remarkable happens. A story is revealed. One story. The story of redemption through Jesus. **This is** *The Gospel Project*.

When we begin to see the Bible as the story of redemption through Jesus Christ, God's plan to rescue the world from sin and death, our perspective changes. We no longer look primarily for what the Bible says about us but instead see what it tells us about God and what He has done. After all, it is the gospel that saves us, and when we encounter Jesus in the pages of Scripture, the gospel works on us, transforming us into His image. **We become God's gospel project.**

Core Values

Deep, but Not Dry

We believe it's best to expect a lot out of those who attend a small group. We don't need to go only as deep as the least knowledgeable person in the group. We may have to "cut up the meat" for new believers and make sure the truth is accessible, but the important thing is that everyone has been fed and is sufficiently nourished.

Christ-Centered

God is the primary Actor in the grand narrative of Scripture, and the gospel of Jesus Christ is the climax of this story. We approach the Old Testament as Jesus did: all the Scriptures testify to Him. We approach New Testament ethics and commands as implications that flow from the gospel—Christ crucified and raised.

Story-Focused

Being Christ-centered naturally brings our focus to the overarching story that the Bible tells in four parts: Creation / Fall / Redemption / Restoration. This helps us connect the dots in the great story that tells the truth about our world and provides a hope-filled outlook on our world because of the future God has promised.

Mission-Driven

Telling the story of the Bible is impossible without leading to mission, as the gospel reveals the heart of our missionary God and His desire to save people of every tribe, tongue, and nation. Keeping a focus on how the gospel leads us to mission is a crucial aspect of how we apply the Bible to our lives.

Introduction

THE GOD WHO IS

In Jesus' high priestly prayer in John 17, we see that the purpose of Christ's work is that He might be glorified and that we might come to know Him. Knowing God, not just knowing about God, is the point of studying theology. The more we know God, the more we will be on mission to make Him known and the more Christ is glorified. Therefore, this study of the doctrine of the Trinity serves to glorify "The God Who Is" and to give fuel for mission in the life of believers.

Chapter 1

Knowing God

The Role of Theology in the Life and Mission of the Christian

---

VOICES FROM *Church History*

"What comes into our minds when we think about God is the most important thing about us."[1]
–A. W. Tozer (1897-1963)

VOICES FROM *the Church*

"A test of your love for God is to examine your love for others."[2]
–Henry T. Blackaby and Richard Blackaby

In life there exists a fundamental difference between merely knowing about something and actually knowing it. Seeing pictures of a safari can never do justice to the experience of coming upon a herd of elephants or catching a glimpse of graceful giraffes on the horizon of the African savanna. Reading *Oliver Twist* is not the same as experiencing life as an orphan. Watching *Saving Private Ryan* does not truly communicate the horrors and heroism experienced at Normandy. There is an essential and marked distinction between merely *knowing about* and actually *knowing.*

Seeing, experiencing, and tasting something truly majestic produces awe and wonder. Nothing is more majestic than God. That is why no encounter should leave us as awed as experiencing Him. Meeting the triune God creates an awed sense of immensity and beauty, what the biblical authors called fear, or reverence. And this fear of God is the beginning of knowledge (Prov. 1:7).

Unfortunately, many contemporary Christians live with relative disregard for God. Casualness characterizes the lives of many believers today. Many have ceased to contemplate God in marvelous awe and wonder and now find their relationship with God marked by disinterested neglect. The sense of beauty and immensity has been replaced by complacency and careless indifference.

God is not boring! He is an infinite and unfathomable abyss of joy and truth. In seeking to know God, we seek our greatest good and eternal pleasure (Ps. 16:11).

In this chapter, we will see that theology is the study of the glory of the triune God as revealed in the gospel. This gospel is the grand narrative of what God has done in Christ that we might know Him. This knowledge permeates every aspect of our being such that our proper response is a desperate mission to know and enjoy Him ourselves and to make Him known and enjoyed by others.

The gospel is about what God has done in Christ that we might know Him (John 17:1-5).

1 *Jesus spoke these things, looked up to heaven, and said:*
Father,
the hour has come.
Glorify Your Son
so that the Son may glorify You,
2 *for You gave Him authority*
over all flesh;
so He may give eternal life
to all You have given Him.

3 *This is eternal life:*
that they may know You, the only true God,
and the One You have sent—Jesus Christ.
4 *I have glorified You on the earth*
by completing the work You gave Me to do.
5 *Now, Father, glorify Me in Your presence*
with that glory I had with You
before the world existed.

John 17, commonly called Christ's "high priestly prayer" is often broken into three sections: His prayer for Himself (vv. 1-5); His prayer for His disciples (vv. 6-19), and His prayer for the church (vv. 20-26). In the first section, the prayer is permeated with the theme of glory.

God loves glory. The glory of God is such a dominant biblical theme that one could make the case that it is the end for which everything exists. God delights to be known and enjoyed.

Furthermore, God's love for His own glory is good news for the world. How is this? Because it guarantees that God will make provision for people to know and enjoy Him! God desires to be known and thus delights to make Himself known.

In one sense, we can say that God displays His glory throughout the universe (Ps. 19:1-6). The cosmos is continually overflowing with hints of the glory of God. Every sunrise and sunset, mountain and valley, and ebb and flow of the ocean tide discloses a powerful and benevolent God. Creation reveals its Creator as a work of art reveals the mastery of the artist.

But there is a deeper and clearer revelation of the glory of God than that found in creation. The ultimate display of the glory of God is not found in nature but rather in the gospel of Jesus Christ.

Imagine staring at a faded photograph. Weather, wear, and time have obscured what once was vibrant. How different is a glimpse of a faint and faded reflection from a personal encounter with the subject of the photograph. This difference is similar to that between the glory of God revealed in creation and that revealed by Christ.

The hints and shadows displayed in creation are insufficient to portray the infinite and perfect attributes of a holy God. When Christ commends a saving knowledge of the triune God, He is speaking of something beyond that which is revealed in creation. He is speaking of Himself.

Notice the focus on Christ's work in verse 4. The work that was given to the Son can be summarized by two words: *revelation* and *redemption*. The Son both reveals and accomplishes the plan of the Father to redeem people to delight in His glory.

The gospel not only reveals the glory of God, but it also enables man to enjoy that glory. The gospel makes the knowledge of God possible by overcoming our inherited blindness and rebellion. The gospel is not merely the content of the knowledge of God, but it is also the instrument through which that knowledge comes to be known.

The gospel—this grand narrative centered on the life, death, and resurrection of Jesus Christ—is the profound final revelation of the knowledge of God. The Person and work of Jesus Christ is the foundation of all true and transformative knowledge of God. In the gospel we see the love of God most clearly, and this vision radically changes our lives. Eternal life consists of the knowledge of God, which is clearly articulated in the gospel of Jesus Christ.

The study of theology is not merely to know about God but to know Him (John 17:6-10).

6 *I have revealed Your name*
to the men You gave Me from the world.
They were Yours, You gave them to Me,
and they have kept Your word.
7 *Now they know that all things*
You have given to Me are from You,
8 *because the words that You gave Me,*
I have given them.
They have received them
and have known for certain
that I came from You.
They have believed that You sent Me.
9 *I pray for them.*
I am not praying for the world
but for those You have given Me,
because they are Yours.
10 *Everything I have is Yours,*
and everything You have is Mine,
and I have been glorified in them.

The pursuit of the knowledge of God is called *theology*. Unfortunately, the term *theology* often gets a bad rap when it is actually an indispensable, inescapable, and enjoyable enterprise.

The term *theology* simply indicates any word, thought, or conception of God. According to Psalm 14:1, the fool states that God does not exist. Such a statement is a theological expression. Though the expression does not correspond to reality, it is nonetheless theological. Everyone is a theologian—Christian, Jew, Mormon, Muslim, Buddhist, atheist, agnostic, etc. We all have certain thoughts, ideas, or conceptions of who God is or isn't. We are all theologians, and every thought is on some level quite theological.

For the Christian, the goal of theology is simple—knowing God. As we have seen, to know Him is to enter into and possess eternal life (John 17:3). It is to embrace and enjoy His glory as revealed in the gospel. Unfortunately, many Christians are content simply knowing about God rather than actually knowing Him. What is the difference?

To begin to answer that, answer this question: What is one thing you have always wanted to see? It could be a natural wonder, such as the Grand Canyon, Mount Everest, or Oahu's North Shore. It could be man-made, such as the Eiffel Tower, Cambodia's Angkor Wat, or the Burj Khalifa in Dubai. Does a quick Google search for images, the reading of a Wikipedia entry, or watching a National Geographic special quench the thirst to experience the majesty of such wonders? If anything, far from satisfying the desire, such study only further intensifies it. One can know quite a bit about a person, place, or thing and yet never truly experience it.

Similarly, when the Bible commends the knowledge of God, it expresses something beyond the acquisition and recitation of facts or mere acquaintance. Knowing God is a more profound and transformative experience than knowing about Him.

The seminary student who can read Hebrew and Greek but whose prayer life and marriage are in shambles proves that width of knowledge does not necessarily translate into depth of knowledge. Tim Keller uses the illustration of a vending machine in which the coin has been put in the slot but has failed to drop. The knowledge of the gospel has been seeded into many minds but sometimes lodges there and fails to drop into the heart.[3]

One can know the Ten Commandments and not obey them. One can memorize the Scriptures and yet not really see through them. As the purpose of a window is that we might not see the window but see something through the window, so the Scriptures are not to terminate on themselves but rather on Him to whom they point. This was Jesus' warning to the Pharisees in John 5:39-40: "You pore over the Scriptures because you think you have eternal life in them, yet they testify about Me. And you are not willing to come to Me so that you may have life."

When Christ commends the knowledge of God, it is an intimate familiarity that is described. The "word" and "name" of God revealed in the gospel are both believed and received (John 17:6-8). This is to be distinguished from mere acquaintance. You know your father, you know your neighbor, and you know your husband or wife, but the depth and intimacy expressed in those differing relationships is profound.

The knowledge of God is more than intellectual. It is emotional and volitional as well. One can memorize the entire Bible and yet remain ignorant of God. One can attend seminary, read Christian classics, attend Bible study after Bible study and yet not really know God.

This should not be taken to indicate, however, that these theological pursuits are to be avoided. It is only by looking through the windows that we see outside the house. In the same way, it is only by reading the Scriptures that we see the Son who images the Father. One cannot know the Father without first knowing about Jesus.

In order to know God, we must surely first know about Him, but we must not stop there. In his contemporary classic *Knowing God,* J. I. Packer asks, "How can we turn our knowledge *about* God into knowledge *of* God?" His response is profoundly helpful: "The rule for doing this is simple but demanding. It is that we turn each truth that we learn *about* God into matter for meditation *before* God, leading to prayer and praise *to* God."[4]

The clearest expression of the loving character of God is found in Christ, and the clearest revelation of the character of Christ is found in the Scriptures. The most obvious and authoritative place to begin with a study of God is in the Bible.

The more we know God, the more we will be on mission to make Him known (John 17:17-23).

17 *Sanctify them by the truth;*
Your word is truth.
18 *As You sent Me into the world,*
I also have sent them into the world.
19 *I sanctify Myself for them,*
so they also may be sanctified by the truth.

20 *I pray not only for these,*
but also for those who believe in Me
through their message.
21 *May they all be one,*
as You, Father, are in Me and I am in You.
May they also be one in Us,
so the world may believe You sent Me.
22 *I have given them the glory You have given Me.*
May they be one as We are one.
23 *I am in them and You are in Me.*
May they be made completely one,
so the world may know You have sent Me
and have loved them as You have loved Me.

There are multiple effects of the knowledge of God upon His people, but we will highlight two in particular: sanctification and mission.

Christ prays for the sanctification of His people. To be sanctified is to be set apart. In some sense, we are sanctified the moment that we believe, but there is also a progressive element to our sanctification. The more deeply we know God, the more truly we begin to resemble Him in His holiness because we are conformed to the image of Christ (2 Cor. 3:18). The more clearly we see Christ, the more we resemble Him (1 John 3:2).

Now look at John 17:20. Christ's prayer was not intended to be restricted to the disciples gathered with Him on the night of His betrayal but indeed for all of those who would subsequently believe. And how were they to believe but through the message of those original disciples? Christ's desire is for the expansion of the glory of the triune God through the proclamation of the gospel by His followers.

Certain moments in history are forever etched into memory. These moments are of various types. Many are of great tragedy, as most Americans recall with vivid detail JFK's assassination, the Challenger explosion, or the fall of the towers on 9/11. Others are momentous occasions of great personal joy, such as the slow walk down the marital aisle, the birth of a child, etc. Still others are corporate reminders of great athletic triumph, as with the U.S. hockey team's 1980 "miracle on ice" or Michael Phelps' numerous medal-winning races in the 2008 Olympics.

Each of those memories capture not only a thought but certain feelings as well. Close your eyes and think back to one of these moments. What were you feeling? What were you thinking? What was happening around you?

Laughter, tears, sorrow, disbelief, joy, and numbness were all natural depending on the context of the occasion. Profound experiences naturally and normally result in profound responses. How strange it would be to visualize those occasions accompanied by disinterested boredom! Imagine trying to stifle your emotions in the midst of such triumph or tragedy. Does it not feel forced and foreign? Something deep within us overflows in that moment and demands to be seen and heard.

C. S. Lewis wrote that praise is a natural and spontaneous result of all enjoyment.[5] In other words, the crowd's applause at a sporting event is not merely some tradition handed down over the centuries or a result of evolutionary development. It is an echo of a reality deeply embedded into who we are as persons. It is a glimmer of a truth about human nature itself. Humans are natural worshipers, and nothing is easier or more natural than praise.

Those who know God best have found this tendency toward spontaneous delight to be true in the realm of the divine. When we encounter the God of the gospel, we experience something profound, and the natural result of that experience is called praise. And this praise delights to be communicated.

In fact, delight is incomplete until it is shared. The heart that is impacted by the love of God on display in the gospel naturally desires to communicate that love with others.

Consider this: When you get good news, what is one of your first instincts? You begin to call friends and family and share the news with them. Why? Because joy is not complete until it is extended. In fact, in sharing the joy with others, your own experience of the pleasure actually increases.

The gospel is this kind of news. As we come to know God in the gospel, we desire to share that knowledge with others. Like Jeremiah, the knowledge of God becomes a fire in our souls burning to be shared with others (Jer. 20:9).

Conclusion

Our mission is to make much of God. Those who truly know God desire to make Him known to others. Since there is no greater knowledge of God than that found in the gospel, we become a people of the gospel who are passionate to make Christ known and enjoyed in this world.

Devotions

Knowing the Father Through the Son

John 17:3: "This is eternal life: that they may know You, the only true God, and the One You have sent—Jesus Christ."

Do you know God? What a profoundly important question. Life or death and eternal punishment or pleasure rest on how you respond to those four words.

Who is God? If you consult an increasingly secular society, you will find many answers. For instance, God is an internal reality or an external principle or power. God is a tree or in a tree. God is nothing. God is dead, as Nietzsche famously declared. The world religions declare that God was once a man like us or that He was revealed finally by Muhammad or that there are many gods. It is impossible to answer the question "Do you know God?" unless one can first identify God. The Bible identifies Him with astounding clarity. God, far from some vague and abstract principle, is perfectly revealed by Jesus Christ.

Irenaeus, an early church father, wrote, "the Son, administering all things for the Father, works from the beginning even to the end, and without Him no man can attain the knowledge of God. For the Son is the knowledge of the Father."[6] To know God means to know the Son of God. There is no true knowledge of God that does not filter through the Son.

This knowledge of the Son begins and ends with the gospel. Christ's incarnation, perfect obedience, crucifixion, resurrection, exaltation, and future return contain infinite mysteries to explore. To have eternal life, we must know God. To know God, we must know Jesus Christ, whom He has sent. To know Jesus Christ, we must know the gospel.

Pause and Reflect

1   How would you answer if someone were to ask you, "Who is God?"

- -

2   What is the logical fallacy in claiming a knowledge of God while rejecting Christ?

- -

3   How has the knowledge of Christ changed your life?

GRAVITY AND GLORY

John 17:4: "I have glorified You on the earth by completing the work You gave Me to do."

The purpose of the gospel is the glory of God. Christ came to glorify God by redeeming people to love and enjoy Him forever. His healing of the sick, preaching to the crowds, calling of the disciples, crucifixion, and resurrection were all designed with a purpose—the glory of the Father. The glory of God is the end for which all things exist.

Since glory is so central to the biblical revelation, we must have some conception of what glory actually is. The Hebrew word for "glory" connotes substance and weight, giving rise to C. S. Lewis' famous essay *The Weight of Glory*. Glory is an all-pervasive reality that surrounds us every day and beckons us to belief and delight.

Do you feel the "weight of glory" pressing down upon your life? Unfortunately, many who call themselves Christians live with disinterested neglect. Far from a blissful weight pressing and influencing everything they say and do (1 Cor. 10:31), the glory of God is nothing more than an afterthought. It is secondary, peripheral, minor. It is nothing more than a brief intermission or interruption.

But God is not weightless. The glory of God is no marginal matter. If all else were trivial, He would still remain substantial and His glorious love central. The glory of God, His weight and gravity—this is why we were created and redeemed, that we might know and enjoy Him forever.

Pause and Reflect

1   How would you define the word *glorify*? What does it mean to glorify God?

- -

2   To what degree does the glory of God influence your daily life?

- -

3   How can you glorify God in eating and drinking? How can you apply this principle to the way you love your spouse and children, the way you do your job, the way you love others, the way you spend vacation, etc.?

A Sent People

John 17:23: "I am in them and You are in Me. May they be made completely one, so the world may know You have sent Me and have loved them as You have loved Me."

Here we are privy to an intimate conversation between the Son and His Father. The Son knows that He is loved. The love of the Father is never questioned. It is always at the forefront of the Son's identity. To be a son is to acknowledge the love of a father.

Not only does the Son know that He is loved but also that He is sent. Sent for what purpose? To glorify the Father through the gathering of people into His kingdom. The Son was loved. The Son was sent. And so the Son went.

As the Father has loved the Son, so has He loved His people. In fact, His love for the world was a motivation for sending the Son (John 3:16). As with the Son, the Father's love carries a calling. Those whom He loves He sends. The work of sending has not ceased.

The sending of God's people is called *mission*. God's mission is the magnification of His glory through the reconciliation of a broken world. We are loved by God and sent by Him to proclaim His goodness and grace to others that they too might know and enjoy His love.

Pause and Reflect

1 Why did God send His Son? Try to identify more than one or two answers to this question.

- -

2 Do you think of yourself as being "sent" as an ambassador of Christ for the reconciliation of the world? In what ways can you better fulfill this appointment?

- -

3 What hinders you from sharing the good news of the gospel?

DISCUSSION QUESTIONS

1 What words would you use to describe your relationship with God? Do you see tendencies toward complacency and indifference in your communion with Christ? If so, what are some of the roots of that condition?

2 Why do you think the knowledge of God we can gain through creation is insufficient for salvation?

3 If someone were to ask you to summarize the gospel, how would you do it? How does the gospel fulfill God's chief desire to be glorified?

4 What words would you use to describe *theology*? Dull, dry, boring, academic? Joyful, exciting, refreshing? Why would you use the words that come to mind?

5 Why might people dislike theological study? What are the dangers of neglecting theology in favor of vague spirituality? Of exalting study at the expense of delight and duty? Where on the spectrum do you most often find yourself?

6 What are some personal moments that reflect the tendency toward overflowing and natural expressions of joy or sorrow?

7 Do you think of evangelism and mission as a spontaneous overflow of joy? If the work of mission feels forced and laborious to you, why do you think that is?

8 What steps can you take to personally and practically pursue knowledge *about* God?

9 What steps can you take to personally and practically translate knowledge *about* God into knowledge *of* God?

10 What has the Lord revealed about your own heart through this study that should lead to confession and repentance?

Part 1

GOD THE FATHER

Before the universe began, before the beginning of time, God existed in His perfection, subsequently displayed to His creation in the works of His hands and in His Word to humanity. He is spirit, all-knowing, all-powerful, and everywhere. He is good and merciful. He is love. He is holy. He is just. And He is jealous for His glory and His people. There is only one God, but the Bible is equally clear that this one God exists in three Persons: God the Father, God the Son, and God the Holy Spirit.

Chapter 2

The God Who Is

The Existence of God

"My argument against God was that the universe seemed so cruel and unjust. But how had I got this idea of *just* and *unjust*? A man does not call a line crooked unless he has some idea of a straight line. What was I comparing this universe with when I called it unjust?…Thus in the very act of trying to prove that God did not exist—in other words, that the whole of reality was senseless—I found I was forced to assume that one part of reality—namely my idea of justice—was full of sense. Consequently atheism turns out to be too simple."[1]
–C. S. Lewis (1898-1963)

VOICES FROM *the Church*

"If you want to know what it means to be a human being, you must look not at human beings but at Jesus Christ. We are broken and corrupted images, but he is the true image of God, the model, the prototype."[2]
–Ben Patterson

Do you remember when you first heard about *The Hobbit* or *The Lord of the Rings*? My college roommate introduced me to the books in the late 1960s. At first his references to hobbits and orcs bewildered me. Then I decided to read *The Hobbit*, and I was hooked. Since then, I've read through *The Lord of the Rings* five times.

As I immersed myself in the stories, I wondered what kind of person came up with such a wonderful, imaginary world. Who was J. R. R. Tolkien? Middle-earth was filled with history and grandeur and characters that break your heart. But what did his literary masterpiece reveal about himself?

In our late-night dorm discussions, we concluded the following: The author believed that right will prevail against all odds. The author was convinced that things happen for a reason. The author appreciated beauty. The author understood that there are powerful forces, even supernatural forces, in the world. The author loved the English language and was a master of creative expression.

Today we can learn in detail what Tolkien was like by reading what he said about himself or by learning from those who knew him. But we can also learn about the creator of Middle-earth by looking carefully at his creation. Consider other works of human genius—the Mona Lisa tells us something about Leonardo da Vinci; the iPhone tells us a great deal about Steve Jobs.

In this chapter, we will focus on the case for God's existence. We start with creation as a pointer to the Creator, then consider the scriptural evidence for God's existence, and finally recognize that all humans have an inner sense that He exists. The goal is that our faith will be strengthened and we will be better equipped to respond graciously to those who deny we can know God.

Creation points to the existence of God (Ps. 8:3-8).

Atheists and agnostics have long been part of the intellectual discourse of Western civilization. Within the past few years, however, a more militant form of atheism, sometimes called "new atheism," has gained traction. Its proponents are intolerant of religious beliefs. They seek to criticize and expose belief in God as irrational. Leading voices in this movement include Richard Dawkins, Sam Harris, and Christopher Hitchens.

A Christian's response to atheism should not be overly defensive or dependent on clever attacks. Instead, we ought to begin by acknowledging that throughout history, almost everyone who has considered the "something" that exists—the universe—has concluded that the universe did not invent itself. As surely as the existence of *The Lord of the Rings* points to an author, so the universe points to a Creator beyond itself.

We can go back all the way to the time of the Old Testament to see this truth. King David was a military genius and a master politician. Furthermore, he crafted amazing Hebrew poems (now known as psalms) on a great variety of subjects. Psalm 8 is one of David's reflections on the Creator and His creation.

3 *When I observe Your heavens,*
the work of Your fingers,
the moon and the stars,
which You set in place,
4 *what is man that You remember him,*
the son of man that You look after him?
5 *You made him little less than God*
and crowned him with glory and honor.
6 *You made him lord over the works of Your hands;*
You put everything under his feet:
7 *all the sheep and oxen,*
as well as the animals in the wild,
8 *the birds of the sky,*
and the fish of the sea
that pass through the currents of the seas.

As we watch David describe what he perceived with his senses, we learn that careful observation of nature is a friend of faith, not a foe. What David saw in the night sky overwhelmed him! He might not have known scientifically just how vast the universe is, but he understood well enough that everything came from the hand of a mighty Creator. It came from His "fingers" as a potter's jar comes from the workman's hands.

The vastness of the heavens was a reason for David to believe God exists. It was not a reason, as some have recently argued, to deny a Creator. Furthermore, David noticed not only the objects of creation ("moon" and "stars") but also their orderliness ("You set in place"). The heavenly bodies point to a purpose—not limited to but no less than the guidance they give to nighttime travelers.

That the apparent design and purpose of many parts of the universe points to a Designer is known as the "teleological argument." The Englishman William Paley (1743-1805) developed the famous watchmaker argument: Just as the existence of a watch, which has a purpose to tell time, presupposes a watchmaker, so the existence of purposefulness in the natural order points to a Creator of that order and purpose. [3]

More recently, certain scientists have used a version of this argument to develop the "intelligent design" movement. Not all of them reach the conclusion that the God of the Bible is the Creator of the universe. They do, however, make the case that certain features of the universe are best explained by an intelligent cause, not by undirected processes such as natural selection. [4]

When David compared the vastness of the universe to himself, he was struck by the smallness of all humanity. Why should the God of the universe pay attention ("remember" and "look after") to humanity? In a famous *Peanuts* comic strip by Charles Schulz, Charlie Brown is standing outside and looking up at the starry night sky. After several moments of silence, Charlie Brown decides to go inside. "I'm beginning to feel insignificant!" he says.

Small, yes. Insignificant, no. David may have wondered at humanity's smallness, but he had seen evidence all around him of humans fulfilling God's call to rule wisely over the earth. He had seen animals domesticated ("sheep and oxen," and David by profession a shepherd). He had seen wild beasts subdued ("animals in the wild," and David as one who overcame lions and bears [1 Sam. 17:34]). His mind went to the air ("birds of the sky") and the waters ("fish of the sea"). Through the centuries, humanity has brought animal life of every kind under dominion.

Even more, this psalm that exults in the magnificence of God and the loving attention that He shows people points forward to Jesus Christ. Humans are creation's crown, and Jesus Christ is the crown of humanity. He is the One crowned with glory and honor—God with us. That's why the apostle Paul quoted from this psalm when speaking of Jesus (1 Cor. 15:27).

Likewise, the author of Hebrews pointed to this passage in his exaltation of Jesus: "For He has not subjected to angels the world to come that we are talking about. But one has somewhere testified: What is man that You remember him, or the son of man that You care for him? You made him lower than the angels for a short time; You crowned him with glory and honor and subjected everything under his feet. For in subjecting everything to him, He left nothing that is not subject to him. As it is, we do not yet see everything subjected to him. But we do see Jesus—made lower than the angels for a short time so that by God's grace He might taste death for everyone—crowned with glory and honor because of His suffering and death" (Heb. 2:5-9).

Psalm 8 is also an early example of what is often called the "cosmological argument" for God's existence. The "teleological argument" looks at design or purpose and sees evidence of a Designer. The "cosmological argument" asks the question "What or who caused the universe in the first place?"

In simplest terms, the cosmological argument runs like this: "Whatever begins to exist has a cause of its existence. The universe began to exist. Therefore, the universe has a cause of its existence."[5]

Arguments and proofs are important. But we must remember that these traditional proofs for God's existence bolster our faith; they do not create it. We do not *argue* people into God's kingdom. Neither do we study these truths merely from an analytical point of view.

We should learn from David's example. Psalm 8 does not begin or end with an intellectual assent to God's existence; David actually worships the Creator: "Yahweh, our Lord, how magnificent is Your name throughout the earth!" (vv. 1,9). God desires not to be analyzed but adored.

Scripture points to the nature of God (Gen. 1:1; Ps. 14:1-3).

Christian apologetics—the case for God, the Bible, salvation in Christ, and so on—often proceeds by beginning with the external evidence. But the Bible itself does not start with an argument for the existence of God. He is simply presupposed as the Creator of all things. This is well illustrated by Genesis 1:1.

1 *In the beginning God created the heavens and the earth.*

There is no explanation of where God came from or how He came to be. It's simply assumed that the God of the Bible is the one true uncreated Creator and Lord of the universe. As has been often preached, once a person accepts Genesis 1:1 as true, everything else in the Bible is possible.

The Bible not only assumes God's existence but also the existence of moral right and wrong. Some people doubt there is a God because of all the bad things that happen in the world. They wonder: *If there is a good God, why do bad things happen?* But in even asking this question, we are pushed back toward God. If there are bad things, good and evil, right and wrong, it must be because there is a God who is the source of good.

We call this line of thinking the "moral argument" for God's existence. In its basic form, the argument looks like this: If God does not exist, then objective moral values and duties do not exist. Objective values and duties do exist. Therefore, God exists.[6]

King David linked proper regard for God with moral behavior in Psalm 14. Disbelieving in God is a moral decision, not just an intellectual decision. David called this kind of person "the fool." He did not mean unintelligent, ridiculous, or easily duped. Rather, he was saying that such a person lacked good sense.

Folly in the Old Testament was the opposite of wisdom (Prov. 1:7). Let's look carefully at the opening verses of Psalm 14:

1 *The fool says in his heart, "God does not exist."*
They are corrupt; they do vile deeds.
There is no one who does good.
2 *The LORD looks down from heaven on the human race*
to see if there is one who is wise,
one who seeks God.
3 *All have turned away;*
all alike have become corrupt.
There is no one who does good,
not even one.

David began by assuming the fool's position: no God exists. Then he showed the inevitable outcome, using negative descriptions: "corrupt" in heart and "vile" in deed. "There is no one who does good," he lamented.

Verse 2 poetically describes God's inquiry into the state of human evil. As "the LORD" (Yahweh, the covenant-making God of Israel), He longed to find someone who was truly wise, one who wholeheartedly sought Him. Alas, God's conclusion was that "not even one" human being has done the right thing.

The psalmist linked belief in a moral God with moral behavior. To deny God's existence is foolish.

But it is not just atheists who are indicted in this passage. What about us? If there is no one who does good, then we are under judgment too! Even if we believe in God, don't we sometimes live as "practical atheists," living day to day as if He does not exist? Real atheists and practical atheists share the following traits:
• They pray rarely if at all.
• They do not read or study the Bible.
• They walk by sight, not by faith.
• They give little or nothing to charitable or Christian causes.
• They live primarily for this life rather than eternity.[7]

In Romans 3, the apostle Paul quoted from this psalm as a way of underscoring how sinful *everyone* is. We cannot put ourselves on a pedestal and look down our noses at those who don't believe in God. The reality of sin levels us all. Thankfully, the grace revealed in the gospel reaches into the hearts of intellectual and practical atheists alike and not only shows us right from wrong but also *declares* us right before God through our faith in Christ's work.

All humans have an inner sense that God exists (Rom. 1:21; Ps. 10:3-4).

So far we have seen the evidence for God from creation itself, touching on two classic proofs for His existence (the teleological and cosmological arguments). We have also considered that the Bible simply assumes God and that the existence of good and evil points to Him (the moral argument). But now we turn to the truth that all persons have a deep inner sense that there is a God and that we are created beings. The apostle Paul made this very case in Romans 1:21.

21 *For though they knew God, they did not glorify Him as God or show gratitude. Instead, their thinking became nonsense, and their senseless minds were darkened.*

In the preceding verses, Paul affirmed that certain aspects of God's nature—His existence and His power—are revealed by the created order. Mankind is thus able to know these things about Him. Further, humans can figure out that they should express appropriate thanks to their Creator ("show gratitude") and worship Him ("glorify Him").

Yet like those condemned in Psalm 14, everyone's natural thinking has gone wrong ("became nonsense"). Further, our ability to make good moral decisions is compromised ("minds were darkened"). It was not that we denied the Creator; far from it. We have taken the intuitive knowledge of God that we had and used it in the wrong way. We turn to idolatry—the worship of created things—rather than the worship of the Creator (Rom. 1:22-23).

You see, denying God is never merely an intellectual decision. The Bible makes the case that we deny or ignore Him to escape accountability for our moral actions. We return again to the Psalms, this time to Psalm 10:

3 *For the wicked one boasts about his own cravings;*
the one who is greedy curses and despises the L ORD.
4 *In all his scheming,*
the wicked arrogantly thinks:
"There is no accountability,
since God does not exist."

The essence of sin is to put self first. We boast about our own cravings and brag about self-achievement (power, possessions, sexual conquests). Untamed greed—the desire for more—ultimately leads a person to curse and hate God.

We turn morality upside down. We should boast in the Lord and despise what is self-centered. But we have done just the opposite.

Thankfully, God's common grace means that human beings still have a conscience. We are not as bad as we could be. Our conscience gives us a sense not only of His existence, His power, and His right to be worshiped but also a sense of guilt and shame when we violate it. What's more, the gospel that God accepts us because of the work of Christ is all the more compelling when contrasted with our own brokenness and shame.

Common grace restrains the unbeliever's heart so that not all the wickedness inside is acted upon. Gospel grace changes the unbeliever's heart so that Christ's goodness overflows into lives of obedience to God.

Conclusion

Understanding the proper relationship between the Creator and the created has often been a challenge, even to believers. When we recognize our smallness in creation, we can better understand the greatness and glory of God. Keeping this perspective will enable us to be involved in creation care. This really matters because there is a Creator. But creation care can become idolatrous. Some people are committed to environmental issues and yet are not committed to the Creator.

Making a case for the existence of God is an important step in evangelism. Still, we must remember that believing in God is *not* enough to save us. It is possible to believe that God exists and yet not have a saving relationship with Him. Yet people must start with accepting the existence of God the Creator before they are ready to hear the good news of the Savior.

Voices from *Church History*

"I do not venerate matter, I venerate the fashioner of matter, who become matter for my sake, and in matter made his abode, and through matter worked my salvation...I reverence therefore matter and I hold in respect and venerate that through which my salvation has come about, I reverence it not as God, but as filled with divine energy and grace."[8]
–John of Damascus (circa 675-753)

Devotions

CREATION'S VASTNESS

We enjoy the same night sky King David celebrated in Psalm 8. What a staggering thought! The city lights where I live dim the Milky Way and keep me from seeing clearly the diamond-filled heavens that those out in the country take for granted. In recent decades, however, we have seen stunning images from the farthest corners of the universe, transmitted by the Hubble Space Telescope. (Three mouse clicks take you to a magnificent slide show.)

Read all of Psalm 8, and try to put yourself in David's place. Imagine him as he experienced the moon while tending sheep, with the regularity of its monthly cycles. I wonder what he made of the fixed stars and constellations like Orion or the Big Dipper. Think of him trying to tease out the mystery of the seemingly random movement of the planets. Did he know that Venus was both the Morning Star and the Evening Star?

Rather than think about the universe in scientific terms ("How big is it? When did it begin?"), consider what the heavens show about the One who designed and created it. David also did that. He made the connection that the Creator of all things is none other than Yahweh, the covenant-making God of Israel. Then he worshiped Him whose magnificent name spreads throughout the earth. In this chapter we dig into how the creation gives evidence of the Creator. Ask God to confirm to you that He—the great Creator—is also the God known through Jesus Christ.

Pause and Reflect

1 If you like scientific explanations for things, why is it important to move from observation to worship?

- -

2 If you are not interested in such explanations, how might scientific knowledge help you appreciate God?

- -

3 What persuades you that the great Creator is also the God known through Jesus Christ?

Living as a Practical Atheist

Psalm 14:1: "The fool says in his heart, 'God does not exist.'"

Sometimes Jesus' followers use such verses to thumb our noses self-righteously at those expressing doubts about God. But recently I have realized that Psalm 14 challenges the way I carry out my daily lifestyle.

I'm pretty decent at "the morning quiet time" thing. I have a pattern of Scripture reading and—depending on how focused I am—working through my prayer list. Then I head out the door for work. I easily lose any connection with the Lord I had enjoyed. Too many times I return in the evening with the uncomfortable feeling that I haven't thought of Him or talked to Him or done anything to acknowledge His lordship during the workday.

Frankly, I'm the one who's the fool here. When I don't consciously depend on the Lord and instead act as if I'm in control and it's all up to me to produce, I'm a practical atheist. I'm living no different than an outright atheist. When I live all day for my career, thinking about saving up for retirement rather than investing in what's eternal, I'm a practical atheist, even if I'm paid for doing Christian stuff.

My challenge and yours is to put God and the gospel first in every situation faced during the day. I know in my head that Christ is my Lord and that He longs for me to acknowledge that He is in charge. Every stoplight, every conversation, every annoyance is an opportunity to prove I believe in God.

Pause and Reflect

1   In what ways are you most prone to live as if God does not exist?

----

2   How do your prayer and Bible study practices reveal that you and almighty God are communicating?

----

3   How does your life differ in practice from that of a kind and generous atheist (and there are some!)?

Living as God's Regent

Psalm 8:6: "You made him lord over the works of Your hands."

David was echoing God's word to our first parents: "Fill the earth, and subdue it" (Gen. 1:28). Humanity stands between God and the rest of creation, serving as His stewards over His creation. The marks of sin show up in the ways people mishandle creation. Yet humans do amazing things, crafting earth's elements into wonderful buildings and precious artifacts. By making things—a poem, a plane, a pie—we fulfill what God has asked us to do.

As Jesus' followers, we long to see His fame spread throughout the world. Surely one way this happens is by making lovely or good things in a way that tells others, directly or indirectly, that we honor our Creator and Redeemer through the works of our hands. J. S. Bach and G. F. Handel affixed the acronym "SDG" (*Soli Deo Gloria*, Latin for "Glory to God alone") to music compositions. Another who showed us a way to do this, even while cleaning pots and pans, was Brother Lawrence, the 17th century Frenchman whose life inspired the classic *The Practice of the Presence of God*.

Consider the day that lies ahead. Perhaps you will be people focused as a teacher or a public servant. Maybe you will work with your hands in construction or on the farm. Perhaps you will sit at a computer sending countless emails or meeting the next project deadline. Pray that the Lord will let you see the ways you can be on mission with Him throughout the day.

Pause and Reflect

1   What do you want others to remember about your accomplishments 10 years after your death?

- -

2   What have you accomplished in life that gives you pleasure that you are God's regent?

- -

3   Think about your primary occupation. How can doing your job well show you are living on mission?

DISCUSSION QUESTIONS

1   What is a work of human culture that you admire or benefit from? What does the maker's work reveal about the character of the maker? How clearly has the maker revealed himself or herself? How else would you learn about the maker?

---

2   How reasonable is it to follow the analogy that just as we can learn about J. R. R. Tolkien by looking at his work, so we can learn about the Creator by studying creation?

---

3   Describe a time when you observed some facet of creation and you were overwhelmed that this was evidence of the Creator. How similar was your reaction to David's reaction to the night sky?

---

4   In what ways does the purposefulness of creation communicate the truth that God has a purpose for humanity?

---

5   To what extent have traditional proofs for God's existence (such as the teleological and cosmological arguments) helped you believe there is a Creator? Have you ever tried to use one of these arguments to help an agnostic or atheist friend? What happened?

---

6   Is it difficult to believe in miracles once you believe in an all-powerful God? How does the existence of God give credence to the stories in Scripture?

---

7   How does the moral argument affect the way you live? Do you think of God as a heavenly observer of your deeds? How does an understanding of the gospel change the way you live in the presence of God?

---

8   What are some things about God's character that are revealed in the Person of Jesus Christ that we would never know otherwise?

---

9   How closely do you connect "the voice within" with your belief that there is a God? Was Jiminy Cricket right to say, "Always let your conscience be your guide"? What are the limits of relying on our consciences to determine right from wrong?

---

10 In what ways does the truth of the gospel encourage you to talk with agnostics and atheists? What tone should you take in those conversations?

Chapter 3

Our Great God

What God Is Like

Voices from *Church History*

"Our greatest claim to nobility is our created capacity to know God, to be in personal relationship with him, to love him and to worship him. Indeed, we are most truly human when we are on our knees before our Creator." [1]
–John Stott (1921-2011)

Voices from *the Church*

"To know an everlasting God is to know that nothing truly good will ever pass away." [2]
–Mark Galli

King Alexander III of Macedon died during his early 30s in 323 B.C. Well known during his life, he reshaped civilization through his military genius. For the first time ever, the world's political center moved westward into Europe. Alexander was the architect of Hellenization, the spread of Greek culture, language, and religion throughout the world. In fact, the Greek speech spread by Alexander's armies became the language in which the New Testament was composed. He is universally recognized as "Alexander the Great." Few humans have equaled his influence.

Through the ages, a small number of human beings have been considered so important that their names have been tagged as "the Great." There was Gregory the Great, an early pope; Catherine the Great, empress of Russia; and in our time, Muhammad Ali, "The Greatest," a heavyweight boxing champion. You can probably think of others.

Today, we throw around superlatives quite often. A decent musical performance is "awesome." A steak dinner is "amazing." The newest video game is "fantastic." The only problem is that when we come across something truly great, we struggle to find bigger and better superlatives to describe it. In other words, only a few things are really great. When applied to persons, "great," in its true significance, means "remarkable in degree or extent, superior in quality or character, influential, distinguished." If that definition is accurate, few persons can truly be great.

In this chapter, we will learn about the greatness of God the Father. His greatness is seen especially in His identity as King and in His attributes of eternality, immortality, and invisibility. The goal of this session is not only to know more about the Father's attributes but to know Him better. And as we see more and more of His greatness, our hearts should overflow with passion to make His great name known.

God is King and Covenant-Keeper (1 Tim. 1:17; Ex. 3:13-15).

Sometimes, our inflated vocabulary can keep us from acknowledging "true greatness." Our society champions the idea that any individual has the potential to be great—a positive if sometimes naïve result of democratic ideals. Because of our society's emphasis on rising to greatness, it's harder for us to understand the kind of greatness that is based on who someone is rather than what they have achieved. We forget that Alexander was born into a royal family, and those circumstances largely affected his greatness. Since we live in a democratic republic, we don't have the cultural experience that leads us to revere monarchs based on their birth into a royal family.

In the world of the Bible, however, things were very different. Ancient Egypt and Babylon had their dynasties. In Israel, King David's descendants ruled from Jerusalem for centuries. Rome's first emperors all belonged to the lineage of Julius Caesar. Greatness and kingdom went together. That's why it comes as no surprise to find the biblical writers borrowing the language of kingship to help illustrate God's greatness.

The apostle Paul understood this concept well. When he wrote to Timothy, his young colleague in ministry, Paul had actually been a prisoner of the infamous emperor of Rome Nero Caesar. Yet rather than emphasize the negative traits of Nero and other earthly kings, Paul chose to describe the God he knew and loved with the language of kingship. Take a look at 1 Timothy 1:17:

17 *Now to the King eternal, immortal, invisible, the only God, be honor and glory forever and ever. Amen.*

In this study, we will highlight the attributes of God that Paul mentioned in this passage. Notice first that Paul's description of God as *King* stands in stark contrast to Nero as king. God is without beginning or end; the dates of Nero's birth and death are well established. God cannot die; Nero died when his secretary helped him commit suicide. God the Father is invisible and reigns over all; Nero was only one of many earthly kings. The name of God is described with terms like glory and honor; Nero's name has been connected with dishonor and shame. See the difference?

Paul's language of kingship didn't come only from Roman culture. He knew the Scriptures. In particular, he knew the Old Testament psalms—ancient songs that portrayed God as King of the universe. According to the psalms, the Lord sits on a royal throne ruling all (103:19). He watches over the whole earth (33:13-14). He is from everlasting (74:12). He is King because He is Creator (95:3-5). He rules with power and glory (145:11-12). He rules in truth and righteousness (96:13).

God's kingship extends through the whole universe and around the world. So great is He that "the nations are like a drop in a bucket; they are considered as a speck of dust in the scales" (Isa. 40:15).

The Israelites, however, recognized God as their King in a special way. They based this understanding on the covenant relationship they enjoyed with God. Today, we think of covenants as a binding agreement between two more or less equal parties, such as at a marriage ceremony. But the covenants between God and humanity show that God Himself initiated such covenants and established the terms of the agreement.

Early on, God established covenants with Noah and with Abraham (Gen. 9:9; 17:2,7). Yet with these covenants, He never explained the meaning of His name—"the LORD" or "Yahweh." Then came Moses' dramatic encounter with Yahweh at the burning bush. Let's listen in on the conversation between Yahweh and Moses in Exodus 3:

13 *Then Moses asked God, "If I go to the Israelites and say to them: The God of your fathers has sent me to you, and they ask me, 'What is His name?' what should I tell them?"*

14 *God replied to Moses, "I AM WHO I AM. This is what you are to say to the Israelites: I AM has sent me to you."* 15 *God also said to Moses, "Say this to the Israelites: Yahweh, the God of your fathers, the God of Abraham, the God of Isaac, and the God of Jacob, has sent me to you. This is My name forever; this is how I am to be remembered in every generation.*

Moses knew about the many gods of ancient Egypt, each with a name revealing something about him or her. Among these were Horus, the falcon-headed god of the sky and the pharaohs; Isis, the goddess of magic, motherhood, and fertility; and Ra, the sun god and creator. But what was the meaning of the name *Yahweh*? That's what Moses was asking.

We see earlier in the Old Testament that Moses' forefathers were already familiar with the name Yahweh (Gen. 12:8; 26:25; 28:13). This implies that when Moses asked God about His name, he was asking, "What does Your name signify?" For the children of Israel, the meaning of names was important because a name revealed something about one's character.

Yahweh's reply to Moses in verse 15 points to His identity as the covenant-making and covenant-keeping God. The Lord had made an everlasting promise to Abraham that he would be the father of many nations (17:4). God had also told Abraham that his descendants would be enslaved for 400 years but that He would set them free from slavery (15:13-14). Now to Moses, God expressed that the meaning of the name *Yahweh* would be forever connected with His fulfilling the covenant promises made to Abraham, Isaac, and Jacob.

Even though Yahweh appeared in connection with a burning flame in a bush, He revealed Himself to Moses as a personal Being, not an abstract force. God makes promises and then He keeps them. He is to "be remembered in every generation" by the name *Yahweh*, the covenant-keeping King of His people who is always true to His word.

God is eternal and immortal (1 Tim. 1:17; Ex. 3:13-15).

When Paul wrote in 1 Timothy 1:17 that God is the "King *eternal*," he used a phrase that focuses attention on the timelessness of God (literally, "of the ages"). God has no beginning or end. Time is, after all, His creation. He sees all time equally.

Scripture unpacks the eternality of God in many passages. One of the most important is Exodus 3:14, in which Yahweh revealed to Moses that His name means "I AM." He exists from before time even began, before there was a *before*, even though it's impossible for us as time-bound beings to conceive what that means. Consider the following passages that declare this truth:

- "From eternity to eternity, You are God" (Ps. 90:2).
- "But You, Lord, are enthroned forever" (Ps. 102:12).
- " 'I am the Alpha and the Omega,' says the Lord God, 'the One who is, who was, and who is coming, the Almighty' " (Rev. 1:8).

When compared to our brief lifespan from birth to death, God's eternity is simply staggering. The longest-ruling of earth's monarchs last no more than a few decades.

Bible students and theologians have pondered deeply the implications of God's eternality. I am no physicist and can't pretend to know much about the scientific understanding of the relationship between space and time. But it seems clear from real physicists that time and space are related. Thus, because God is the creator of space, He is also the creator of time. He is timeless in His own being.

Furthermore, God's eternality means He sees all time as equally vivid. This is one way of making sense of biblical prophecies. As the psalmist declared, "In Your sight a thousand years are like yesterday that passes by" (Ps. 90:4). At the same time, God wonderfully acts in time. For example, He sent His Son, Jesus Christ, at just the right time. And in due time, His Son will return and make all things right.

The eternality of God helps us understand other aspects of who He is (His attributes) and what He does (His actions, especially in saving us). For example, closely related to "eternity" is "immortality." In 1 Timothy 1:17, Paul described God as "the King eternal, *immortal*." The term translated "immortal" carries the idea of "without death." In other words, God has life in Himself. In His own being, He is fully alive. He is self-existent.

Not only is God immortal, He is also independent. He does not need us or anything else in all creation. He is self-sufficient.

The apostle Paul boldly declared this truth to the religious leaders of Athens: "The God who made the world and everything in it—He is Lord of heaven and earth and does not live in shrines made by hands. Neither is He served by human hands, as though He needed anything, since He Himself gives everyone life and breath and all things" (Acts 17:24-25).

Yet God was pleased to create the universe even though He didn't need it. He made the world to reflect His glory and share in His joy. And thankfully, although sin has marred the universe, God is able and willing to restore it to its original purpose.

This is part of what Moses learned at the burning bush. Yahweh, whose name means I AM WHO I AM, is the God who made covenant promises to Abraham, Isaac, and Jacob that He will fulfill. His self-sufficiency means that His mission will succeed. Life will triumph over death!

Because He is self-sufficient—unlike any gods imagined by mankind—God's purposes cannot fail. As the eternal, immortal One, Yahweh will see to it that "the creation itself will also be set free from the bondage of corruption" (Rom. 8:21). He guaranteed the success of His plan by entering our fallen world in the Person of Jesus Christ, who is Himself eternal and immortal: "Life was in Him, and that life was the light of men. That light shines in the darkness, yet the darkness did not overcome it" (John 1:4-5).

What lessons can we take away from God's eternal nature and immortality? First, any notion that God is beholden to us is shattered. Our life comes from His life. He chose to create. He chooses to use us. But He does not need us any more than oceans need ships or mountains need climbers. The truth of God's eternal nature crushes any sense that God owes us something.

Second, these attributes are great confidence builders. The success of His mission is not in doubt, whether thought of in terms of the spread of the gospel to all people or in terms of the closely related mission of glorifying Him forever. Our salvation and role as those He has included in His mission are absolutely secure. And as we learn more about the Father's attributes, we are motivated to join Him in His mission to make Himself known to others.

God is spirit (1 Tim. 1:17; John 4:24).

We come to focus on another truth that adds to our understanding of the Father's greatness: He is spirit, not material. Paul expressed this concept in 1 Timothy 1:17: "The King eternal, immortal, *invisible.*"

In Jesus' encounter with a Samaritan woman beside a well, He made the following dramatic declaration, recorded in John 4:24:

24 *God is spirit, and those who worship Him must worship in spirit and truth."*

Jesus and the Samaritan woman were discussing the proper location to worship God. If God is physically limited to a spatial location, then the place matters greatly, doesn't it? But Scripture teaches that we must not think of God as having size or dimensions. He is not infinitely large; He exists without materiality. Neither is He some kind of pure energy or pure thought.

Have you noticed how much we've been talking about what God is *not*? He is *not* mortal; He is *not* visible; He is *not* material. But it's not enough to simply talk about what God is *not*. We must also affirm the positive side—what God is. And John 4:24 tells us clearly that God is spirit.

Recognize that this issue of God as spirit is separate from the doctrine of the Holy Spirit, one of the Persons of the Godhead. Later sessions in this volume will explore the person and work of the Holy Spirit. We ought also to note that God has given us spirits in which to worship Him, but we need to steer away from any Greek philosophical notions that the best human form of existence is as disembodied souls or spirits. The Bible is clear that redeemed humans are destined for material existence forever in resurrection bodies as we worship our God who is spirit. Our material resurrection existence will follow the pattern of Jesus' (1 John 3:1-3).

Why is the truth that God is spirit so important? Because those who deny that God is spirit will seek to represent Him materially. And God forbids the creation of idols: "Do not make an idol for yourself, whether in the shape of anything in the heavens above or on the earth below or in the waters under the earth. You must not bow down to them or worship them" (Ex. 20:4-5). To use any part of the created order—earthly or heavenly—to depict God's being is to misrepresent Him and to think of Him as other than He really is.

So when the Israelites made a carved image of God as a golden calf, they may have wanted to show that in His attributes God is strong and full of life (like a calf). But to imply that God in His being was like a calf was to deny equally important characteristics such as love, mercy, and righteousness. Although God has made the material creation so that its parts reflect something of who He is, it dishonors Him to picture Him as existing in such a form.

Why is God so opposed to misconceptions about His nature? Because when we worship Him rightly, He receives glory and we are filled with joy. But when we worship Him wrongly, we make a mockery of His glory and our souls are unsatisfied.

The Lord based the prohibition against images of Himself on His jealousy to protect His honor: "I, the LORD your God, am a jealous God" (Ex. 20:5). He longs for His people to think of Him as He really is. So He is rightly angry when He is falsely represented by a material image. God is spirit. His is the greatest, most excellent existence possible.

Conclusion

Alexander the Great was known to his people through physical representations. Statues of him were erected throughout his realm. Coins were struck bearing his image. These were all meant to help people know his greatness. With our sovereign Lord, things are very different. He is so great that in His essence He cannot be adequately represented by any material depiction.

Long ago, theologian Anselm of Canterbury (circa 1033-1109) developed an important argument for the existence of God (the "ontological argument"). He formulated the saying: God is "that [Being] than which nothing greater can be conceived."[3]

In this study, we have been reflecting on some of the ways in which God's greatness is unsurpassable. Truly He is great beyond our ability to comprehend. Furthermore, each of His attributes of greatness calls us to respond in some way:

• He is King. We are therefore His subjects (and He would have us as willing citizens, not as rebels to be subdued).

• He is covenant-keeper. We are therefore in a binding relationship to Him as the One who has made sure promises.

• He is eternal, existing outside of time. We are therefore His time-bound creatures, dependent on Him to unfold His plan.

• He is immortal, with life in Himself. We are therefore mortal, and if by faith we receive eternal life, we still utterly depend on Him for our life.

• He is spirit; He is invisible and not material at all. We are therefore able to worship Him rightly only when we worship Him through the spirit He has given each one of us.

Devotions

WHAT'S IN A NAME?

In Shakespeare's *Romeo and Juliet*, Juliet asks, "What's in a name? That which we call a rose/By any other name would smell as sweet." From one viewpoint, it's the substance, the content of someone's character that matters, not the tag by which they are called. Thus, when we named our baby, we chose a name that we liked the sound of. Although we scanned "name your baby" books, the meaning of the name was secondary.

But from another perspective, what if there is another way, a better way, to think about names? What if there were a way to connect the character or attributes of a person with the name itself? In the Bible, some important characters had their names changed to reflect who they were. God changed Abram's name to Abraham (from "exalted father" to "father of a multitude"). Jesus changed Simon's name to Peter (from "hearing" to "rock"). Similarly, recall that the angel announced that Mary's baby would be named Jesus (the Greek form of the Hebrew name Joshua) because He would save His people from their sins.

Because God is God, He has chosen His own name; furthermore, His name is not subject to change. Thus, when He revealed that His name is "Yahweh," meaning "I AM," He was explaining that He always is. His name is forever "I AM WHO I AM": "This is how I am to be remembered in every generation" (Ex. 3:14-15). So if we reframed the opening question to "What's in God's Name?" the answer is "He reveals the essence of His being in the name He has chosen."

Pause and Reflect

1   Why does it matter that we understand the meaning of God's name?

- -

2   If you were to give yourself a name expressing your character for the last 20 years, what would it be?

- -

3   If you were to name yourself according to how you see the gospel impacting your life, what would your name be?

Good News: God Is Eternal

As we study God's greatness in this chapter, we see Paul emphasizing that God is "the King eternal, immortal." This attribute of God means something much different than the eternity of the redeemed (an endless experience of time). We'll learn that God exists apart from time. He created time when He created space. Thus, He knows the end from the beginning of all things. He is the Alpha and the Omega, the Beginning and the End—and He is present at all points in between.

Because God exists apart from time, His plan to save sinners has always existed—before there was a "before." In John 17:24, Jesus spoke of His Father's perfect love for Him "before the world's foundation." In 1 Peter 1:20, we learn that "[Jesus] was chosen before the foundation of the world but was revealed at the end of the times for you." So because God is eternal, there can never be any doubt that His marvelous plan of salvation will succeed.

When I am tempted to doubt that God will complete the work He began in me, these texts come to my rescue. I stop striving, and instead, I rest in the eternal God because He has saved me for my good and His glory. It overwhelms me that the love Jesus enjoyed with the Father before there was time extends to us as well: "I made Your name known to them and will make it known, so the love You have loved Me with may be in them and I may be in them" (John 17:26).

Pause and Reflect

1   Have you ever considered what it means that God exists outside time? How do you conceive of this?

- -

2   Are you too time bound? What does your own future eternity imply about how you should live today?

- -

3   How does the truth that God's eternity is part of the gospel encourage you today?

Sent by Our Great God

Whenever we study passages in the Bible about God's greatness, we usually see them end with the persons addressed going on mission. After Moses' dramatic encounter at the burning bush, God sent him to challenge Pharaoh and the gods of Egypt. The result was that Yahweh won a great victory. Word spread throughout the world that the God of Israel had defeated the gods of the world's greatest civilization.

After the Samaritan woman met Jesus at the well, she went back to town, telling her fellow citizens about the greatness of the One she encountered. Many of them believed in Jesus as a result of her testimony. There's no account of her later in the Gospels. We do know, however, that after the day of Pentecost, Philip preached in Samaria, and many persons believed and were baptized.

Timothy was fulfilling his calling as a gospel ambassador to Ephesus when he received Paul's letter that reminded him that God is the "King eternal, immortal, invisible" (1 Tim. 1:17). Timothy continued faithfully in that charge until Paul wrote him another letter asking him to join him in Rome (2 Tim. 3:21). Years later, the congregation of Ephesus was still known for good works and commitment to truth (Rev. 2:1-3).

So it is with us. When we are gripped by the greatness of God, enthralled with the glory of our King, we can't help but tell others about Him. We can't help but join in the joyful challenge of making His fame known. Just as it's the most natural thing in the world for a lover to tell others of his beloved, so it's the most normal thing for us to tell others of God's greatness.

Pause and Reflect

1   Do you identify more with Moses, who resisted being sent by God, or the Samaritan woman, who couldn't help telling her town about the Messiah? Why?

----

2   How would you express the relationship between grasping God's greatness and telling someone else about Him?

DISCUSSION QUESTIONS

1   Do you personally know someone who deserves the title of "great"? What makes them worthy? What factors are considered when people describe world leaders, singers, or athletes as "great"? What does it take for someone to be considered worthy of the title "great"?

2   How does the biblical picture of God as King help you understand His greatness? What negative baggage about earthly kings do you need to overcome in order to appreciate the truth of God's kingship?

3   What do God's actions in relation to the covenant teach us about His character? How does God's mission to rescue His people put on display His attributes?

4   Why is it important to understand God's greatness in terms of eternity? What things keep you from living with a sense of eternity in your heart every day?

5   How is God's eternity different than the eternal life that believers will enjoy?

6   How would you describe God's ultimate mission? In what ways does God's immortality (life, self-sufficiency) give you confidence in your desire to join His mission?

7   Why is it in our best interest to keep ourselves from idols (1 John 5:21)? What does it mean to worship God in spirit and truth?

8   What is the difference between saying that God's attribute of sovereign rule is like that of a king and depicting God the King as a statue of a crowned human male?

9   How does God's mission manifest the attributes we have been looking at today?

10   It's easy to find examples expressing the bad idea that God needs people, either to accomplish His purposes or to somehow make up for a perceived lack in Him. Discuss how to combat such inappropriate expressions as "God needs me to do this."

Chapter 4

The Omni God

God's Omniscience, Omnipresence, and Omnipotence

Nineteen Eighty-Four, George Orwell's novel about a dystopian civilization, puzzled me when I first read it. Back in the 1970s, the thought of everyone in society being under constant surveillance via telescreens ("Big Brother is watching you") didn't make sense to me. I couldn't imagine the technology it would take to make this happen. So I blew it off as doom and gloom. I knew "Big Brother" had entered popular speech as a phrase referring to abuse of government power and repression of civil liberties. But such a thing couldn't really happen, could it?

Fast forward to the 21st century. The technology has been perfected. Surveillance cameras are everywhere. Wherever there are smart phones, videos can be uploaded and viewed instantly all over the world. The Big-Brother-like surveillance of *Nineteen Eighty-Four* doesn't seem so unrealistic anymore.

Most people have a natural terror of Big Brother. We want our privacy. We don't want to be watched. At least in our inner thought lives, we keep a closet where we hide a lot of junk from others and maybe ourselves. So when we think about God and learn that He knows everything about us, it gives us pause. That's why we need to think biblically about what it means for God to be all-knowing and present everywhere.

In this chapter, we will examine three attributes of God. He is all-knowing (omniscient), all-present (omnipresent), and all-powerful (omnipotent). God's omniscience exposes our sins to Him and shows us our need of a Savior. It also means that He knows what lies ahead; nothing surprises Him. God's omnipresence may seem oppressive (there's no getting away from Him!) until we are in Christ and sense the comfort of His presence with us as we engage in His mission. His omnipotence means that He can judge and condemn; it also means that He is mighty to save. His power enables us to do His work, which will be fulfilled.

God is all-knowing—omniscient (Ps. 139:1-6).

What does the Bible actually teach about what God knows? A great place to begin is Psalm 139. The author, David, was reflecting on what he had come to understand concerning this important truth.

1 *LORD, You have searched me and known me.*
2 *You know when I sit down and when I stand up;*
You understand my thoughts from far away.
3 *You observe my travels and my rest;*
You are aware of all my ways.

4 *Before a word is on my tongue,*
You know all about it, LORD.
5 *You have encircled me;*
You have placed Your hand on me.
6 *This extraordinary knowledge is beyond me.*
It is lofty; I am unable to reach it.

Notice that the psalmist began not by remarking on God's factual knowledge of things open to observation, such as "The hairs of your head are all counted" (Luke 12:7). Rather, he started by noting God's knowledge of intimate, personal, relational information: "You have…known me." Further, it was the Lord, Yahweh Himself, whom David was addressing.

David used a variety of verbs to express God's knowing: "know," "understand," "observe," and "are aware." These verbs pile on top of each other to get across the truth that God exhaustively knew everything there was to know about David. God knew his daily rhythms: "sit down…stand up." God knew his thinking, even when it had no words: "thoughts from far away." God knew his speech before it was uttered: "before a word is on my tongue." God knew his activities: "travels…rest…all my ways." The sentence in verse 5 translated "You have encircled me" is literally "Back and front, You enclosed me."

Everything in the psalmist's life was under God's all-seeing eye. He could only respond in light of his own limited knowledge: "This extraordinary knowledge is beyond me." This stands as an expression of David's awe and wonder as well as a recognition of his personal limits. That's why he added "I am unable to reach it."

Bible students have long used the Latin-based term *omniscience* to refer to God's knowledge of all things. This truth is affirmed in many passages. Job's friend Elihu called God "Him who has perfect knowledge" (Job 37:16). The apostle John said God "knows all things" (1 John 3:20).

Even more, Scripture affirms that God's knowledge extends from what is actual even to what might have been. For example, Jesus asserted that the cities of Tyre and Sidon would have repented if His miracles had been done there (Matt. 11:21). God knew what would have happened if the circumstances had been different.

The first response to God's omniscience (for those of us who recognize how flawed we are) is outright terror. The psalmist hinted at this by noting that God had encircled him or hemmed him in, as other translations render the verb. The second response, though, should be wonder. God knows everything about us, and yet He still loves us. He still desires our salvation.

When I try to wrap my mind around the concept of God's infinite knowledge of all things, a number of thoughts come to mind. For example, I realize that if He has always known everything, then He knows everything about Himself. He has never had to second-guess Himself or His motives: "I am God...I declare the end from the beginning, and from long ago what is not yet done, saying: My plan will take place" (Isa. 46:9-10). God's plans are always based on His own perfect knowledge.

Second, if He has always known everything, then what I have done—or will do—cannot take Him by surprise. He knew exactly when I would be born, what experiences I would have, and how my life would unfold.

This truth should strike fear and wonder in our hearts. Fear because God knows all our sin. Wonder because God loves us anyway. Fear because God is in control in a way that is unfathomable to human reason. Wonder because God's knowledge of the future means that none of my trials or difficult circumstances are a surprise to Him.

God is everywhere—omnipresent (Ps. 139:7-10).

As we have already seen, Psalm 139 teaches that God knows all things and is present everywhere. Note how David further explored the amazing truth that God is omnipresent:

7 *Where can I go to escape Your Spirit?*
Where can I flee from Your presence?
8 *If I go up to heaven, You are there;*
if I make my bed in Sheol, You are there.
9 *If I live at the eastern horizon*
or settle at the western limits,
10 *even there Your hand will lead me;*
Your right hand will hold on to me.

David emphasized again the relational aspect of God, this time concerning His presence. The questions he asked in verse 7 have a one-word answer: *Nowhere.* He was persuaded that he could never get away from God's presence. He understood that this could be a great comfort and blessing: "Your hand will lead me." But God's presence could also grip Him: "Your right hand will hold on to me."

Bible students use another Latin-based term, *omnipresence*, to refer to the truth that God is everywhere. He is unlimited in respect to space, just as He is unlimited in respect to time. Because God is spirit, His manner of existence is different from ours. So when we say that God is omnipresent, we do not mean that He is like some giant cloud of gas. If that were the case, then part of God would be in one place and part of Him in another. Rather, all of God is completely present in all places, just as all of God is completely present in all times. Paul affirmed this in Acts 17:28: "In Him we live and move and exist."

All this implies that God cannot be confined to any space, no matter how vast: "Even heaven, the highest heaven, cannot contain You" (1 Kings 8:27). We can never escape His transcendent presence, even in death. We cannot run away from Him in order to hide from Him.

God was present with our first parents in the garden of Eden to bless them. After they rebelled, they tried to hide, but His pursuing presence found them (Gen. 3:8-9). The reluctant prophet Jonah foolishly supposed He could run away from God's presence (Jonah 1:3). The prophet Jeremiah recorded the Lord's words about His presence: "'Am I a God who is only near'—this is the LORD's declaration—'and not a God who is far away? Can a man hide himself in secret places where I cannot see him?'—the LORD's declaration. 'Do I not fill the heavens and the earth?'—the LORD's declaration" (Jer. 23:23-24).

Though God is present everywhere, we don't always have a sense of God's presence. For example, when we gather for corporate worship, we often pray for God to be present. But to be more precise, we are actually praying for His presence to be manifested in a palpable way. The doctrine of omnipresence means that He is already there.

Further, even when we experience God's manifested presence, we do not experience His "face"—His majestic, unveiled glory. That's why, when Moses asked to see the Lord, he was told, "You cannot see My face, for no one can see Me and live" (Ex. 33:20). When David prayed, "Do not banish me from Your presence" (Ps. 51:11), he was asking to regain a sense of God's blessing upon himself. Perhaps the most astonishing divine promise of what the eternal state will be like comes in Revelation 22:4: "They will see His face." Just think about it. In the resurrection, the marks of sin and the limits of mortality will be so diminished that at last God's people will fully enjoy what the old saints called "the beatific vision."

So how do we move from thinking about a weighty topic such as omnipresence to the implications it has for us? As followers of Christ committed to be on mission, *first* we are to be aware that God is with us whether we sense His presence or not. We are not to worship only when we sense that He is near. We are to worship, trusting He is present no matter what feelings we may or may not have.

Second, we rejoice that the risen Lord Jesus gave a special promise of His presence when He gave the commission to make disciples of all nations: "Remember, I am with you always, to the end of the age" (Matt. 28:20).

Third, it is always right for us to walk in a manner worthy of the Lord Jesus (Col. 1:9-14), so that we can ask Him to be near, empower our obedience, receive glory from our work, and bless us as He works through us.

God's Presence in Hell?

At this point, some have an objection to God's omnipresence; "What about hell?" they ask. "Isn't hell about the absence of God? Isn't part of the idea of hell about being banished forever from God's presence?"

The best answer is that *God is present in different ways in different places.* Sometimes He is present to bless His people: "In Your presence is abundant joy" (Ps. 16:11). Sometimes He is present to judge and punish evil: "If they conceal themselves from My sight on the sea floor, from there I will command the sea serpent to bite them...I will fix My eyes on them for harm and not for good" (Amos 9:3-4). Sometimes He is present to sustain His creation: "By Him all things hold together" (Col. 1:17).

Some have used passages such as 2 Thessalonians 1:9 to argue that those condemned to damnation at last get away from God's presence: "These will pay the penalty of eternal destruction from the Lord's presence and from His glorious strength." But the term "eternal destruction" means everlasting ruin, not annihilation. And the phrase "from the Lord's presence" does not mean that He is absent. Those in hell experience God's everlasting presence in judgment. They are separated from Him only in the sense that they can never hope for any change in their miserable condition.

This understanding of God's omnipresence, then, should motivate our efforts to proclaim the good news of Jesus Christ far and wide. In believing this gospel, people come under the blessing of God's presence rather than the judgment of His presence, recognizing that Jesus endured the judgment of God's presence in order for sinners to share in the blessing of His presence.

God is all-powerful—omnipotent (Matt. 19:23-26).

God is infinite in power. The Latin-based term *omnipotence* combines two words: *omni*, meaning "all," and *potens*, meaning "strong, powerful." The Bible affirms in many passages that God has the power to do whatever He decides to do, for "Our God is in heaven and does whatever He pleases" (Ps. 115:3).

Jesus emphatically affirmed this in Matthew 19:23-26:

23 *Then Jesus said to His disciples, "I assure you: It will be hard for a rich person to enter the kingdom of heaven! 24 Again I tell you, it is easier for a camel to go through the eye of a needle than for a rich person to enter the kingdom of God."*

25 *When the disciples heard this, they were utterly astonished and asked, "Then who can be saved?"*

26 *But Jesus looked at them and said, "With men this is impossible, but with God all things are possible."*

In the immediate context, Jesus was talking about the difficulty with which persons—especially the rich—can be saved. He was affirming what is found throughout the Old Testament: "Nothing is too difficult for You!" (Jer. 32:17). After his ordeal, Job confessed, "I know that You can do anything and no plan of Yours can be thwarted" (Job 42:2).

It's important in thinking about this teaching to note that strictly speaking, there are some things God cannot do. God cannot do anything that is contrary to His character. He cannot lie, for example (Titus 1:2; Heb. 6:18). He cannot tempt someone to do evil (Jas. 1:13). So we must say that God's infinite power is qualified by His other attributes, such as His righteousness and truthfulness.

When Jesus agonized in the garden of Gethsemane, He affirmed that God's power is expressed only by what God wills to do: "All things are possible for You. Take this cup away from Me. Nevertheless, not what I will, but what You will" (Mark 14:36).

God's exercise of His omnipotence over creation is another way to refer to His sovereignty. As King, He exercises rule over all He has made. God's omnipotence means that His ultimate plan for the world cannot be thwarted. The reality of His power means that people will be saved and His mission will be accomplished.

Confidence in our all-powerful God should be the foundation of our joining Him in His work. The reason we do good deeds and share the gospel is not because the power to save people lies in our own efforts. Instead, we go forward on God's mission because the power to save lies in Him. He is the One who is mighty to save. We are witnesses to His power. When we proclaim the gospel, we become the instruments by which Christ accomplishes His mission of seeking and saving the lost.

Conclusion

This study focused on God's *omni* attributes. It is certainly an incomplete presentation of His character. Later sessions will round out the picture so that we also understand God's goodness and love as well as His holiness and righteousness. This study alone may not have dispelled the idea of God as a menacing "Big Brother," always knowing, always present. But let's think about the wonderful aspects of these attributes as we relate to God personally.

First, God's omniscience stands in stark contrast with our limited—and often faulty—knowledge of ourselves, of God, and of others. Yes, God has made us so that we can have true knowledge. But we will never attain anything like omniscience, even in glory. Thank God that He knows Himself as He truly is. Thank God that He knows us as we truly are.

When we realize that He knows us, including our sins, this may make us want to hide from Him. But if we run to Jesus Christ instead of hiding, we find Him forgiving us despite our sins. He chooses to save. Furthermore, we can rest assured that now that we have been forgiven, God knows us as beloved sons and daughters. He knows our past. He knows our present. He knows our future. Still He loves us and calls us His own.

Second, God's omnipresence stands in contrast to our limited presence. As human beings, we are limited to the place where our bodies are. But God is present in all places. Forever He sustains His creation. Forever He is present either to bless or to punish. His pursuing presence is a fearful truth when we try (unsuccessfully) to hide from Him. But when at last God finds us (not that He was ever far away), we see that He is present with us to bless. And the presence of Jesus Christ through the Holy Spirit undergirds the mission He has called us to.

Third, God's omnipotence stands in stark contrast with our puny abilities. When we are united with Him and His purposes, His power is available to us. By His great power, He has saved sinful people like you and me. His kingdom mission—announced in the Great Commission (Matt. 28:18-20)—will be accomplished. Nothing is too difficult for Him.

Devotions

MEDITATION ON PSALM 139

This study of God's "omni" attributes focuses on the first 10 verses of Psalm 139. We investigate what this psalm teaches theologically about God's knowledge and power. At the same time, it is good to remember that David set forth these truths in the context of his personal experiences. Furthermore, he expressed truth as a prayer—not a bad thing to do. Thus, take the time to read all of Psalm 139 slowly as an expression of your own personal prayer. Ask God to make David's experiences real for you as well. Keep the following outline in mind:

1. Prayer confessing Yahweh's personal knowledge of the psalmist, including all thoughts (vv. 1-6).
2. Prayer confessing Yahweh's presence everywhere, from which there was no escape (vv. 7-12).
3. Prayer acknowledging Yahweh as his Creator, down to the last detail and last day of life (vv. 13-16).
4. Devotion to Yahweh, who judges evildoers but leads the upright to the everlasting way (vv. 17-24).

If you mark your Bible, take time to circle or note all the references to "God" or "Lord," including "You" and "Your." Next, mark all the verbs that indicate actions God has already completed (ex. "searched," v. 1). Observe how David called on God to exercise His power (in judging evildoers) for the sake of His reputation; Yahweh is not the sort of deity who will let rebels against Him go on forever (vv. 19-22). Finally, note that the psalmist ended by expressing complete devotion to this wonderful God. He was confident that if He turned to God in trust, his offenses would be identified and removed. So he boldly prayed, "Lead me in the everlasting way" (v. 24).

Pause and Reflect

1   Does David pray as one who would escape God if he could or as one who delights in God or both? Why?

- -

2   How close are you really to being able to join David in asking God to thoroughly search you?

THE GOD OF THE IMPOSSIBLE

God's power to do what is impossible focuses on what looks to be impossible from a merely human viewpoint. Thus, when the virgin Mary was confronted with the news that she would become pregnant and give birth to a son, she rightly asked, "How can this be?" (Luke 1:34). Through natural processes, there can be no such thing as a pregnant virgin. But with the God of the impossible, it's another matter.

Think also about the possibility of death being reversed. In ordinary experience, this can't happen. But in the case of Jesus, "God raised Him up, ending the pains of death, because it was not possible for Him to be held by it" (Acts 2:24). Furthermore, because Jesus has become the firstfruits raised by God from death, so all who are in Christ have the promise of future resurrection (1 Cor. 15:20-28).

This same principle applies to how we become right with God. From a human point of view, there's no hope. Good works aren't able to save, "for no one will be justified in His sight by the works of the law" (Rom. 3:20). Wealth isn't able to save, "for it is easier for a camel to go through the eye of a needle than for a rich person to enter the kingdom of God" (Luke 18:25). When Jesus' disciples responded to this teaching in dismay—"Then who can be saved?"—Jesus replied with an astonishing declaration of God's power to do the humanly impossible: "What is impossible with men is possible with God" (18:26-27).

Just think about it. Your right standing with God is all because He has done what is impossible!

Pause and Reflect

1 Why is it important to compare God's power to what is humanly impossible?

----

2 What humanly impossible thing would you like to ask God to do in your life? Your church's life?

RESPONDING TO GOD'S OMNISCIENCE

When I was little, my mom tricked me into thinking she had eyes in the back of her head. I believed she could see everything I did. This was her way of keeping me in line even when she wasn't present. Now, as a parent myself, I know how far she was from seeing everything, just as I am far from seeing my own son all the time. Yet for God, seeing everything is true, not a trick.

What must it be like for God to know absolutely everything? Such thoughts quickly lead me to recall my own limited, partial knowledge—of myself, of God, and of others. Through the prophet Isaiah, the Lord declared, "For as heaven is higher than earth, so My ways are higher than your ways, and My thoughts than your thoughts" (Isa. 55:9).

God knows me much better than I know myself. He knows the good things about me. He knows the sinful things about me. This works in two directions. On one hand, before I was a believer, I had a much higher opinion of my goodness than God did. He saw what a rebel I was against Him. He knew (and still knows) the dark places that need the light of Christ to be applied to them. Only when His Spirit convicts me of sin will I repent (John 16:8-11).

On the other hand, now that I believe, it's possible to have false guilt, not fully comprehending the extent of God's forgiveness and my reconciliation to Him: "Even if our conscience condemns us, that God is greater than our conscience, and He knows all things" (1 John 3:20).

Pause and Reflect

1   Think about your life in the past 24 hours. What is the best thing about God knowing all about it? What is the worst thing?

- -

2   Is there some past part of your life in which you have not fully received God's forgiveness?

DISCUSSION QUESTIONS

1   Have you ever experienced "Big Brother"—government or institutions intruding into your private business and repressing your liberty? Does the thought of God seeing everything you do comfort you or concern you? How is God different than an impersonal "Big Brother" telescreen?

2   Why is it important to think of God's omniscience in personal, relational terms? What emotional response do you have when you realize that God knows everything about you?

3   How does God's exhaustive knowledge of all things help you interpret the circumstances of your life? Why should a Christian take comfort in God's omniscience?

4   If God is everywhere, why do we as Christians pray for God's presence in our worship services? What is it we mean when we ask God to be present with us?

5   In our technological age, we are often present physically but distracted by devices so that our minds are somewhere else. How is our prayer life affected knowing that God is never distracted, that He is always listening?

6   In what ways can we become more aware of God's constant presence? How does knowing about God's omnipresence motivate us in our mission to help people come under His blessing rather than under His judgment?

7   Does God share His power with us? How does God's power enable us to fulfill His mission?

8   In what ways does the truth that God cannot do certain things (things that contradict His character) give us even more reason to trust Him? What is the connection between God's unchanging character and His omnipotence?

9   As a result of this study, which of the three *omni* attributes is the most difficult for you to accept or understand? Which one is the most comforting for you?

10 In what ways could you change your attitudes and actions so that you are more aware of God's wonderful knowledge, presence, and power?

Chapter 5

Good God

The Goodness and Love of God

VOICES FROM *Church History*

"Lord of hosts! When I swim in the merciful waters of your grace I find that I can neither plumb nor measure the depths."[1]
–Menno Simons (1496-1561)

VOICES FROM *the Church*

"The very fact that a holy, eternal, all-knowing, all-powerful, merciful, fair, and just God loves you and me is nothing short of astonishing."[2]
–Francis Chan

Once while I was driving on the interstate, my car was struck hard by a vehicle that had lost control. The impact knocked the left rear wheel and brake assembly off my car. I glimpsed my tire spinning into the right shoulder as I passed out of control across three lanes of heavy traffic. By the time I could react, my car slid to a stop in the left emergency lane. Wonder of wonders, I was not scratched, nor was the driver of the other vehicle.

During the next 24 hours, I relived those harrowing seconds a thousand times. I saw the event as a remarkable example of God's providence to me—clearly He wanted me to live, for at least another day! And that has been a comfort indeed. But even beyond my amazement at God's providence, I have been overwhelmed with gratitude for His goodness.

In this chapter, we will see what it means to affirm that God is good. In particular, we will see how His goodness is displayed in His acts of mercy (goodness to those in distress) and in His acts of love (goodness in giving Himself to others). We will see that God is always good in His character, purposes, and actions. He expresses mercy toward humans by providing relief for both physical and spiritual suffering. His self-giving love is the basis for our salvation and the motivation for our loving God and others as we show the world God's love through our actions and words.

God is good (Ps. 106:1-5).

The English word *good* is complicated. When applied to persons, it may refer to the idea of moral excellence ("The teacher had a good influence on her students"). It may also mean physical attractiveness ("The teacher was good-looking"). I counted at least 20 different connotations of *good* in an Internet search. So what are we talking about when we say that "God is good"?

When we say "God is good," we mean that everything God is and does is worthy of approval and that He Himself is the final standard of determining what is worthy of approval.[3] From the beginning, Scripture has affirmed this understanding of His goodness: "God saw all that He had made, and it was very good" (Gen. 1:31).

In a way, everything that is truly good should be worthy of our approval. But what if our evaluation differs from that of another? There must be some external or objective standard for determining good. Ultimately, we as created beings are not totally free to decide by ourselves what is worthy of approval and what is not. That's why we must affirm that God Himself is the standard of good.

That said, goodness is not a standard that exists above or outside of God. Rather, who He is defines what good is. The Bible teaches that He is the source of everything good: "Every generous act and every perfect give is from above, coming down from the Father of lights" (Jas. 1:17). He does only good things for His children: "He does not withhold the good from those who live with integrity" (Ps. 84:11), and "We know that all things work together for the good of those who love God" (Rom. 8:28).

Psalm 106 is a biblical text that teaches us something about God's goodness. Take a look at the first five verses:

1 *Hallelujah!*
Give thanks to the LORD, for He is good;
His faithful love endures forever.
2 *Who can declare the LORD's mighty acts*
or proclaim all the praise due Him?
3 *How happy are those who uphold justice,*
who practice righteousness at all times.
4 *Remember me, LORD,*
when You show favor to Your people.
Come to me with Your salvation
5 *so that I may enjoy the prosperity*
of Your chosen ones,
rejoice in the joy of Your nation,
and boast about Your heritage.

Did you notice the two parallel terms used in this psalm to describe God's character? "Good" and "faithful love." These two descriptions were such a powerful representation of God that His people sometimes spoke of them as if they were alive and in pursuit of human beings: "Only goodness and faithful love will pursue me all the days of my life" (Ps. 23:6). How wonderful it is to think of the sheer goodness of God hunting us without ceasing until we have been pierced by His arrow of love!

God's good character leads Him to purpose good toward others and to act in accordance with His goodness. Thus, He performs "mighty acts" on behalf of His people. These mighty acts culminate in "salvation" and "prosperity"—that is, spiritual and material wholeness.

In turn, those who have enjoyed His goodness are to extend it to others. For example, such persons "uphold justice" and "practice righteousness" because in His goodness God always acts from His justice and righteousness.

The psalmist couched his human response to God's goodness in terms of the collective experience of Israel as God's "chosen ones." They were "Your people," "Your nation," and "Your heritage." This reminds us that as Jesus' followers, we experience God's goodness not only as individuals but also in community with others.

One of the greatest privileges we have is to worship God as a gathered body of believers. We "give thanks." We "proclaim all the praise due Him." We "rejoice" and "boast" in our good God. The first word of the psalm is "Hallelujah!" which means, "Praise Yahweh," a reminder that it is never enough just to know about God's character. We are to respond with praise.

If praise and worship mark our vertical response to God's goodness, then our horizontal response is to do good to others. Thus, Paul challenged the believers in Galatia: "So we must not get tired of doing good, for we will reap at the proper time if we don't give up. Therefore, as we have opportunity, we must work for the good of all" (Gal. 6:9-10). Because we humans are naturally selfish and not good, it's only as we have been transformed by God's goodness that we truly extend goodness to others.

God is merciful (Ps. 106:6-12).

When God's goodness comes in contact with particular situations, it can be more specifically defined using other important biblical terms. For example, *mercy* is His goodness toward those in misery or distress. Thus, I experienced His goodness as mercy in the distressing car wreck I described earlier.

The Lord's quality of mercy causes Him to respond both to physical misery and to spiritual misery as well. Scripture affirms His mercy in many places. He proclaimed to Moses, "Yahweh is a compassionate and gracious God, slow to anger and rich in faithful love and truth" (Ex. 34:6). David proclaimed, "As a father has compassion on his children, so the LORD has compassion on those who fear Him" (Ps. 103:13).

At the same time, it's important to emphasize that mercy (like grace) is freely given. God is not obligated to express mercy. He declared, "I will be gracious to whom I will be gracious, and I will have compassion on whom I will have compassion" (Ex. 33:19). Thus, should I have been maimed or even killed in my car wreck, I could not complain about a failure of divine mercy. God's goodness always prevails, even when He chooses not to extend mercy in a particular situation.

As Psalm 106 develops, the thought turns from describing God's goodness (in verses 1-5) to a particular occasion in which He displayed mercy (in verses 6-12):

6 *Both we and our fathers have sinned;*
we have done wrong and have acted wickedly.
7 *Our fathers in Egypt did not grasp*
the significance of Your wonderful works
or remember Your many acts of faithful love;
instead, they rebelled by the sea—the Red Sea.
8 *Yet He saved them because of His name,*
to make His power known.
9 *He rebuked the Red Sea, and it dried up;*
He led them through the depths as through a desert.
10 *He saved them from the hand of the adversary;*
He redeemed them from the hand of the enemy.
11 *Water covered their foes;*
not one of them remained.
12 *Then they believed His promises*
and sang His praise.

Human beings don't always respond in the right way to God's goodness. As an Israelite, the psalmist recalled the shameful history of his people. God had mercifully done "wonderful works" and "many acts of faithful love" in bringing Israel out of Egypt (see Ex. 7–13). Yet the people immediately "rebelled by the sea" against Him (see 14:10-12). They complained that God had led them out of Egypt so they would die in the wilderness. Such rebellious attitudes did not belong only to the past. The psalmist included himself and his own times: "we and our fathers have sinned."

The psalmist believed God's merciful salvation flowed from His very character, that is, He saved them "because of His name." Yahweh had determined "to make His power known." The psalmist rooted his thinking in the historical situation that birthed his nation. Today, however, we can be just as confident that all God's saving acts flow from His character in order to make His name famous.

In verses 9-12, the psalmist recalled God's mercy to His rebellious people through their crossing of the Red Sea. As a result, they "believed" in Him ("The people feared the LORD and believed in Him and in His servant Moses," Ex. 14:31). Then they "sang His praise" in the exuberant song of Moses (Ex. 15).

Verses 7-12 express a typical pattern in which God displays His mercy in the presence of human sin and rebellion: God acts faithfully toward persons. Persons still rebel against Him. God then acts to redeem sinners. The redeemed believe Him and praise Him.

Those who have truly received God's mercy in salvation are inevitably changed by it. If their God has been merciful to them and they have been changed by His mercy, then they necessarily seek to express mercy to others. In the Sermon on the Mount, Jesus proclaimed, "The merciful are blessed, for they will be shown mercy" (Matt. 5:7). This suggests an ever-increasing cycle. When we as sinful individuals receive God's mercy, we show mercy to others. And then others reflect mercy back to us. And then we extend more mercy. And so on.

What if we do not show mercy? The implication of Jesus' teaching is that if we stop showing mercy, we may not really understand what mercy is. Furthermore, there may come a time when no more mercy will come our way—either from others or from God Himself.

God is love (1 John 4:8-11).

The culmination of God's goodness is His love. Although we typically think of love as an emotion (and thank God for the feelings of love that we have all enjoyed!), the love of God is best understood as His eternally giving of Himself to others. Even before the creation of the universe, when only God existed, there was perfect love among the Persons of the Trinity. Jesus prayed, "Father...You loved Me before the world's foundation" (John 17:24). God alone loves with absolute freedom.

Unfortunately, many today understand the love of God as a kind of mushy sentiment. God is thought to be a kindly old grandfather who tolerates naughty children as long as we aren't too vicious. One reason for this misunderstanding is that *love* (like *good*) can be used in so many different ways, everything from "I love cotton candy" to "I love my country" to "I love Jesus."

C. S. Lewis' highly acclaimed book *The Four Loves* teased out different ways of understanding the love we experience as human beings.
(1) "Affection"—the natural fondness for family members or other persons that comes about through familiarity.
(2) "Friendship"—the bond between persons who share common interests or activities.
(3) "Eros"—the emotional attraction of "being in love."
(4) "Charity"—the supreme, self-giving love that is characteristic of God Himself and gives direction to the other loves. [4]
Lewis was clear that the greatest love was "charity," a term that corresponds to the primary use of "love" in the New Testament to communicate the specifically God-like virtue described by "God is love" and "God loved the world in this way: He gave His One and Only Son" (John 3:16).

God's love as expressed to His human creatures is an expression of His goodness. It extends to His enemies, but it was a costly love. God gave Himself in sacrificial love by sending Himself in the Person of His Son. Thus, this biblical teaching on the love of God is expressed well in 1 John 4:8-11:

8 *The one who does not love does not know God, because God is love.* 9 *God's love was revealed among us in this way: God sent His One and Only Son into the world so that we might live through Him.* 10 *Love consists in this: not that we loved God, but that He loved us and sent His Son to be the propitiation for our sins.* 11 *Dear friends, if God loved us in this way, we also must love one another.*

In this passage, the elderly apostle John, possibly the last of Jesus' original 12 disciples still alive, was writing to believers to explain the nature of God's love.

First, note what he did not write in verse 8. He did not say that God is *only* love. Love is an important attribute of God, but He has numerous other attributes, such as omnipresence (see the previous chapter) and holiness (see the following chapter).

Second, he did not write that love is God. Unfortunately, people can make love an all-consuming idol, such as a mother who overprotects a child or a man who terrorizes or imprisons a lover.

In verse 9, John declared the essence of God's love. It is not an abstract idea. It is not a mushy feeling. He revealed His love in the costliest way imaginable: "God sent His One and Only Son into the world." Of course, John was speaking of the incarnation; God put on human skin in the Person of Jesus Christ. Note how John developed the particulars about God's love:

The Source of God's Love

God loved not because of anything lovable or lovely in humanity. John was explicit: "not that we loved God." Paul put it even more bluntly: "But God proves His own love for us in that while we were still sinners, Christ died for us!" (Rom. 5:8). So the basis of God's love is simply God's love.

The Cost of God's Love

In using the phrase "the propitiation for our sins," John included a world of insight. In one way, the phrase stands as a summary of all the suffering and death of Jesus. Yet the word "propitiation" is very telling. It is a rich word that means "a sacrifice that bears God's wrath and turns it to favor."[5] As the perfect sacrifice for our sins, Jesus took away the well-deserved wrath of God by bearing the punishment of our sins.

The Result of God's Love

John wrote that those who receive God's love "live through Him." John was referring not to biological existence; rather, he meant everlasting life, the spiritual quality of life that begins when someone is born again (John 3:5-15). Furthermore, he implied in verse 8 that those who receive this love actually know God. Just think about it—God loves us so much that He provided a way for us to know Him personally.

The Overflow of God's Love

Love can't be hoarded. "If God loved us in this way, we also must love one another." In other words, persons who lack love show that they have never been changed by the gospel. This repeats John's thought from verse 8: "The one who does not love does not know God."

We began this study by considering God's goodness. All He is and does is worthy of approval. Then we moved more specifically to His mercy—His goodness to those in distress. Finally, we have considered His love, His giving of Himself to others, in particular His giving of Himself in the Person of Jesus as the propitiation for our sins so that we may have life.

When we focus on God's self-giving love, we see that it is the basis for our salvation. It is the motivation for our loving God. It is the motivation for our loving others. We show the world that God is love, that He is good and merciful, by our own love-prompted actions and words.

Conclusion

Let me return briefly to the automobile accident I mentioned at the beginning of this study. I spoke of it as a specific instance of God's goodness to me, and indeed it was. I could just as easily have spoken of it as an instance of mercy, for I was thrown into deep distress and He had compassion and rescued me physically. Furthermore, I could just as well have spoken of His great love in sparing me, and it was that as well. (Although, to be sure, it was not as great as His love for me in sending Jesus to be my Savior!)

But let me now turn the tables from these attributes as God has expressed them to me to how I am to reflect them to others. Because I have experienced the sheer goodness of God—beyond counting blessings—I have the wonderful opportunity and responsibility to do good to all (Gal. 6:10). Because I have received God's mercy, God intends for me to extend to others the mercy I have been shown. And because I have experienced that God loves me, a sinner, then "if God loved us in this way, we also must love one another" (1 John 4:11).

Devotions

AND IT WAS VERY GOOD

Genesis 1 famously recounts God's creation of the world. We often read this chapter to learn about God as Creator or about humanity as created in His image. Or we use it to debate different theories about the age of the world. But one of the author's main points was to show God's goodness in everything He did. Take a look at the passage. It's striking to note the seven times "good" is mentioned (vv. 4,10,12,18,21,25,31).

All these things were good because they came from the Creator, who is Himself good. The first thing that was not good was the loneliness of the man (2:18), so in His goodness, God made woman.

But instead of acknowledging that everything God was and did was good, they rejected Him, and sin entered the world. The rest of the Bible is the story of God's active work to restore His creation to a state of goodness. The apostle Paul had this in mind when he wrote, "The creation itself will also be set free from the bondage of corruption into the glorious freedom of God's children" (Rom. 8:21).

Look around at elements of nature you can see: a bush, a pet, a glass of drinking water. All such things may be tainted: a bush can be full of thorns; a pet can bite; water can be polluted. But they all still bear marks of being part of the creation that God declared "good."

Pause and Reflect

1   Think about your life in the past 24 hours. How have you enjoyed the goodness of God in creation?

- -

2   A popular saying is "God is good all the time. All the time God is good." Is this a helpful word for you or has it become trite? How might you rephrase it to be more memorable for you personally?

CONFESSION OF SIN AND DIVINE MERCY

This study of God's goodness and mercy focuses on Psalm 106:1-12. These 12 verses are just the first part of a long psalm that recounts the nation of Israel's many rebellions against God. The Lord's mercy is even more staggering in light of everything the people did to despise His kindness. Take time to read through the entire psalm, noting especially the concluding verses (vv. 47-48).

The psalmist believed that he and his people had not yet run out of mercy from God, and surely this was true. He ended with a triumphant note of praise. He could not fully know that the greatest overflow of mercy would arrive with the coming of the Messiah. Centuries later, at the birth of the Messiah's forerunner (John the Baptizer), the baby's father, Zechariah, understood. When he praised God in song, he borrowed from Psalm 106. Compare the psalm and Zechariah's song:

Psalm 106:10: "He saved them from the hand of the adversary; He redeemed them from the hand of the enemy."
Luke 1:71: "Salvation from our enemies and from the clutches of those who hate us."

Psalm 106:44-45: "He took note of their distress, remembered His covenant with them."
Luke 1:72: "He has dealt mercifully with our fathers and remembered His holy covenant."

It is when we are most conscious of our sins—and therefore of our need for repentance and confession—that we are most ready to receive divine mercy. Mercy can never be demanded, but we can plead for it.

Pause and Reflect

1   When was the last time you consciously reflected on past sins that God in His mercy has forgiven?

----

2   Are you up to date in confession? If it has been a while, stop to recount your sins and plead for mercy.

----

3   How confident are you that God's mercy is greater than your sins?

LES MISÉRABLES

The musical version and movie adaptations of Victor Hugo's magnificent *Les Misérables* have become a worldwide phenomenon. Near the beginning, the story illustrates how transforming mercy can be. When the hardened criminal Jean Valjean was released from prison, he was welcomed into the home of a kind bishop. During the night, Valjean stole some silver and escaped. The next morning, the French police brought him back to the bishop's door with the silver as evidence. One word from the bishop and Valjean would be back in prison for life.

The bishop exclaimed words to this effect: "Here you are! I'm glad to see you. Did you forget that I gave you the candlesticks too? They're silver and worth a lot of money. Why did you forget to take them?" Valjean was astonished. The police withdrew, and the bishop insisted on giving the candlesticks to him. He was transformed and became an honest man, extending mercy to others.

This is a story of mercy: goodness toward someone in distress. The mercy of God was mediated through the bishop, but this is how we all ought to act. When we have received and understood God's mercy given through Jesus Christ, we are transformed. Then we extend it to others, who in turn are transformed. "But God, who is rich in mercy, because of His great love that He had for us, made us alive with the Messiah even though we were dead in trespasses" (Eph. 2:4).

We are on a mercy mission. We show mercy because He first showed mercy to us. We extend the good news of forgiveness because we stand forgiven.

Pause and Reflect

1   Can you think of another illustration of life-changing mercy from popular culture?

- -

2   In what recent situation have you been very aware of the need to extend mercy to another?

- -

3   Pray for God to open your eyes to a mercy mission opportunity during the next 24 hours.

DISCUSSION QUESTIONS

1   What are some ways we use the word *good* in common conversation?

----

2   Have you ever gone through a crisis that turned out good in the end? What emotions did you experience at that time and afterward? Have you gone through a crisis that did not turn out well? Were you still able to recognize God's goodness to you? Why or why not?

----

3   Why are praise and thanksgiving to God essential responses to His goodness? Describe the experience of corporate worship among people who have benefited from God's mighty acts.

----

4   Name some specific ways you can work for the good of all as a demonstration of God's goodness to you. How can you move from sentimentality to decisive action to show God's goodness?

----

5   What does it say about human nature that we often respond wrongly to God's expressions of goodness to us? What is necessary for us to respond rightly?

----

6   Describe how the merciful heart of God leads us to show mercy to those in need. What biblical examples can you think of? In what specific way could you show mercy to someone in distress or need?

----

7   What are some dangers in thinking that God is only love? How do these dangers keep us from an accurate picture of who God is?

----

8   Is it really possible to decide to love someone and then act on that decision? Or does love between human beings depend on spontaneous emotion? How could you imitate God's love specifically for someone today?

----

9   Some people truly seek to display God's mercy; others are not truly seeking God's mercy but only want to feel spiritual. How can we tell the difference? Why is the distinction important?

----

10 Some Bible students believe that God's love is His greatest attribute. As a result of this study, do you agree with this assessment? Why or why not? What specific action step will you take to demonstrate to another person God's goodness, mercy, and love?

Chapter 6

Holy, Holy, Holy

God's Holy and Righteous Character

VOICES FROM *Church History*

"God is sovereign, so live confidently. God is holy, so live reverently." [1]
–Adrian Rogers (1931-2005)

VOICES FROM *the Church*

"The god who is truly scary is not the wrathful God of the Bible, but the god of the judgmentless gospel, who closes his eyes to the evil of this world, shrugs his shoulders, and ignores it in the name of "love." What kind of "love" is this? A god who is never angered at sin and who lets evil go by unpunished is not worthy of worship." [2]
–Trevin Wax

Jealousy is an emotion we've been acquainted with ever since we were little kids. It's a central theme in countless children's stories. For example, the stepmother in *Cinderella* is jealous of the attention her husband gives his daughter. After the father's death, Cinderella is treated shamefully because of her stepmother's envy.

Then there is *Snow White*. The wicked queen is jealous of the beautiful girl described as "the fairest one of all." Jealousy leads to murderous plotting. Even newer stories like *Toy Story* build on the theme of jealousy. Woody, the old-fashioned toy cowboy, becomes jealous when his owner, Andy, prefers playing with shiny, new Buzz Lightyear.

It's not just children's stories either. In Shakespeare's *Othello*, the title character is filled with jealousy at the thought of losing his wife Desdemona. And Iago, the consummate villain in literature, envies Othello's prestige to the point he wreaks unmitigated evil.

Even though we usually think of jealousy as a negative emotion (the "green-eyed monster"), we recognize there are times when jealousy is right. For example, a wife is properly jealous if she sees her husband giving romantic attention to another woman. And that's the kind of jealousy we see in God. He becomes angry when His people give their attention to other gods—or when mere things or persons occupy the throne in His people's hearts.

In this chapter, we will see how the holiness of God undergirds all of His other attributes. His holiness forms the basis for His righteous character, His commitment to justice, and His jealous love for His people. It's important for us to understand God's holy justice in order to make sense of the jealous love through which He pursues us in the gospel. God's love for us then becomes the motivating force for our joining Him in His mission of seeking and saving the lost.

God is holy (Ps. 99).

The idea of something being holy rarely enters most people's minds nowadays. For many, saying something is "holy" is like saying it's "sacred" or "numinous"—something that fills our hearts with awe and compels us to investigate it. Think of the biblical scene with Moses and the burning bush. Or the movie scene where Indiana Jones discovers the holy grail. We think of something as holy when it is awe-inspiring and sacred. The biblical concept of God's holiness is not less than this, but it is much more.

God's holiness is so important, in fact, that it is the only one of His attributes affirmed in triplicate. He is declared to be "holy, holy, holy" (Isa. 6:3; Rev. 4:8). He is never said to be "love, love, love" or "great, great, great." So what is it about God's holiness that is so foundational?

In the Scriptures, whenever a person, place, or thing—other than God—is described as *holy*, it generally means "separated from ordinary use and intended for divine or religious use." A good example is the Book of Leviticus, which gives strict guidelines for sacrifices (animals set apart for God), the priesthood (men set apart for God), and holy days (times set apart for God).

But what does it mean to affirm that God is holy? Just this: He is entirely separated from sin.[3] Notice there is a relational aspect to this definition. He is separated from sin or evil. God's holy character means that He distinguishes the holy from the unholy. He asks His people to do the same.

Notice also the moral aspect of this definition. He is separated from what? Sin or evil. He hates sin because it is an affront to who He is. The very name of the third Person of the Godhead is Holy Spirit, a reminder of both these aspects.

One of the Bible's passages that showcases God's holiness especially well is Psalm 99.

1 *The Lord reigns! Let the peoples tremble.*
He is enthroned above the cherubim.
Let the earth quake.
2 *Yahweh is great in Zion;*
He is exalted above all the peoples.
3 *Let them praise Your great*
and awe-inspiring name. He is holy.
4 *The mighty King loves justice.*
You have established fairness;
You have administered justice
and righteousness in Jacob.
5 *Exalt the Lord our God;*
bow in worship at His footstool. He is holy.
6 *Moses and Aaron were among His priests;*
Samuel also was among those calling on His name.
They called to Yahweh and He answered them.
7 *He spoke to them in a pillar of cloud;*
they kept His decrees and the statutes He gave them.
8 *Lord our God, You answered them.*
You were a forgiving God to them,
an avenger of their sinful actions.
9 *Exalt the Lord our God;*
bow in worship at His holy mountain,
for the Lord our God is holy.

This psalm celebrates the holiness of Yahweh in many ways. First, note the triple declaration of verses 3,5,9: "He is holy…He is holy…The LORD our God is holy." Closely related to God's holiness is the sense of awe it provokes: "The peoples tremble." Even nature responds: "Let the earth quake." One can never truly encounter our holy God and be emotionally untouched.

There's more! Notice how God's holiness cannot be separated from His sovereign rule. Whatever sacred spaces He has designated on earth, they are merely the "footstool" for the universal King. Not only that, a holy God has a right to set apart persons to serve Him. The psalmist named Moses, Aaron, and Samuel, each of whom God specifically called into divine service.

What should our response to God's holiness be? Exuberance! "Let them praise Your great and awe-inspiring name"; "Exalt the LORD our God." After all, every glorious attribute of God is to be understood in light of His holiness. He is holy love. He is holy greatness. He is holy mercy. And so on. Furthermore, He is wholly other. When humans are confronted with His holiness, God's purity blazes forth in contrast to our impurity.

It's no surprise that God's holiness was displayed through the rituals He mandated for Israel's worship. The priests were set apart. Ordinary people could never approach God's presence directly. The process was daunting. Yet with the coming of Jesus the holy One, human beings can be made holy and fit for His presence. Because of Christ's work, all believers—not just the super pious—are called "saints," or holy ones (Rom. 1:7; Eph. 4:12).

Because of Jesus, the holiness of God has become for us a source of delight rather than of fear: "He does it [that is, disciplines us] for our benefit, so that we can share His holiness" (Heb. 12:10). Ultimately, there will be a day when everything on earth will be holy: "On that day, the words HOLY TO THE LORD will be on the bells of the horses…Every pot in Jerusalem and in Judah will be holy to the LORD of Hosts" (Zech. 14:20-21).

God is just (Ps. 99).

God's justice is directly related to His holiness. When we speak of God's *justice*, we are referring to the truth that He always does what is right and that He is the final standard of what is right.[4] In other words, God never sins, and He alone determines what sin is.

From Genesis forward, God's justice is affirmed. Abraham appealed, "You could not possibly do such a thing: to kill the righteous with the wicked, treating the righteous and the wicked alike. You could not possibly do that! Won't the Judge of all the earth do what is just?" (Gen. 18:25). In Moses' final song, he wrote, "The Rock—His work is perfect; all His ways are entirely just.

A faithful God, without prejudice, He is righteous and true" (Deut. 32:4). And the same is true in the New Testament: "Christ also suffered for sins once for all, the righteous for the unrighteous" (1 Pet. 3:18).

Now look back at Psalm 99 for a moment. Do you see the close relationship between God's holiness and His righteousness/justice?

- Immediately after the first affirmation that "He is holy" comes the ringing declaration that God the King "loves justice" and "established fairness" (vv. 3-4).
- The only parts of the psalm addressed directly to the holy God ("You…") concern His administering justice and righteousness (v. 4) and forgiving His people while avenging their sin (v. 8).
- As the sovereign, righteous, holy Lord, He gave His people "His decrees and the statutes" (v. 7).
- In His justice He becomes "an avenger of…sinful actions" (v. 8).

In defining God's justice, we noted that He Himself is the final standard of what is right. This parallels what we observed in the previous study about God's goodness. Just as He is the standard of what is worthy of approval (good), so He is the standard of what is morally correct (just). It is a necessary outcome of His justice for Him to treat people according to what they deserve. He must punish sin because it does not deserve to be rewarded. It deserves punishment.

This leads us to consider God's wrath, a theme often mentioned in Scripture. Because God loves everything that is right and that conforms to His holy character, He necessarily hates anything opposed to His holiness. Wrath does not mean that God gets peeved or that He has fits of anger. Rather, His wrath is His *settled disposition against sin*.

What about when God doesn't seem to punish sin? Does this mean He's unjust? The answer must be no, for two reasons. First, another of the divine attributes is patience. Yahweh is "slow to anger" (Ps. 103:8). The apostle Paul reasoned that God's patience and delay in expressing wrath "is intended to lead you to repentance" (Rom. 2:4). But that does not mean He will delay forever: "Because of your hardness and unrepentant heart you are storing up wrath for yourself in the day of wrath, when God's righteous judgment is revealed" (2:5).

Second, God does not punish someone for their sins if some other means of punishing sin is available. This is exactly what the death of Jesus was. In His death, He received divine punishment for our sins. God's righteousness was displayed because He did punish sin; His grace was displayed in that He now forgives people for their sins (3:26).

The Old Testament speaks of the possibility that "righteousness and peace will embrace" (Ps. 85:10). The good news is that in Jesus Christ, they do.

How should Jesus' followers respond to God's wrath? First, we need not fear it anymore. The gospel means that our Savior carried away the wrath of God due to us: "He Himself is the propitiation for our sins, and not only for ours, but also for those of the whole world" (1 John 2:2).

Second, we are to praise God for His wrath. Just think how terrible it would be if God did not hate sin! If this were not the case, He would either enjoy sin or not be troubled by it. If either of these were true, then He would be unworthy of our praise. We rightly imitate God's wrath when we feel hatred against sin and injustice. [5]

As those reconciled to God, Jesus' followers are now in a position to work for justice in our world. Our God is just. We who were unjust are now righteous through Christ. Because we are no longer alienated from God, we follow Him in His deep commitment not only to personal justice but also to justice in society. In many ways, the biblical call to seeking justice in our world is summarized in what Jesus called the second most important command: "Love your neighbor as yourself" (Mark 12:31; see Lev. 19:18).

God's concern for right relationships in society is evident throughout Scripture. The Book of Leviticus—the holiness book—includes multiple guidelines for caring for the poor through the "social welfare" custom of gleaning (19:9-10). It also teaches the importance of "blind justice," not favoring the rich over the poor (19:15). It speaks of showing respect for both the elderly and foreigners (19:32-34).

One of the central messages of the prophets was for the Israelite people to return to righteous dealings with each other: "Seek justice. Correct the oppressor. Defend the rights of the fatherless. Plead the widow's cause" (Isa. 1:17). The New Testament continues this emphasis: "Pure and undefiled religion before our God and Father is this: to look after orphans and widows in their distress and to keep oneself unstained by the world" (Jas. 1:27).

God is jealous (Ex. 34:14).

As we have seen, God in His very nature is both holy and righteous. As sinful creatures, we are unholy and unrighteous. Yet the amazing truth is that through Jesus' work on our behalf, we have been declared holy ("saints") and righteous.

But that is not all. We are called to be like our God in these ways! He is holy; therefore, we as His people are to be holy and to pursue holiness. He is just; therefore, we His people are to pursue righteousness in all our dealings, both personally, in our church lives, and in society.

Now, however, we come to God's jealousy. Are we to be jealous or not? What about Paul's teaching that "love does not envy" (1 Cor. 13:4)?

Although jealously is often a negative emotion in human beings, it can have a positive sense. When Paul wrote, "I am jealous over you with a godly jealousy" (2 Cor. 11:2), he meant that he was protective of these believers. He was seeking their honor and welfare.

This is the bridge to understanding God's jealousy. He is concerned with His own honor. He is concerned when His people give their attention and affection to something or someone other than Himself. Thus, His command for the Israelites not to bow to idols is best understood as God's desire for His people to worship Him wholeheartedly instead of false gods. In Exodus 34:14, Yahweh spoke through Moses:

14 *You are never to bow down to another god because Yahweh, being jealous by nature, is a jealous God.*

We can think of divine jealousy in two ways. First, in humans as well as in God, we can easily distinguish between being jealous *of* someone and being jealous *for* someone. Thus, husbands are properly jealous for their wives. (And if the wife is unfortunately giving attention to another man, then the husband may be jealous of the other man and express the jealousy either properly or sinfully.) God is properly jealous for His people, wanting the best for them.

Second, for God, jealousy may also be understood as His continually seeking to protect His own honor. [6] For humans, this kind of jealousy is wrong. We are to be humble, not proud, not seeking our own glory. But that is because we do not deserve the honor that belongs only to God. It is right for God to seek His own honor, for He alone deserves it.

VOICES FROM *Church History*

"When we merely say that we are bad, the 'wrath' of God seems a barbarous doctrine. As soon as we perceive our badness, it appears inevitable, a mere corollary from God's goodness." [7]

–C. S. Lewis (1898-1963)

As believers, we share God's glory only in a secondary and reflected way, as the moon reflects the glory of the sun (2 Cor. 3:18). When we realize that God deserves all the honor and glory from His creation, then His jealousy when His creatures do not seek His glory is perfectly splendid. He is worthy of all praise, and when we realize this, we are near the heart of genuine worship.

So God is jealous for His glory. God loves His people, and He is jealous for them. In His jealous love, He has pursued rebels and turned them into worshipers. This is the motivation for His mission in the world. This is the motivating force for our work in the world: to see the honor of God's name spread ever farther and farther. This compels us forward in doing good and sharing the good news of Jesus to those who have fallen short of the glory of God.

Conclusion

The beginning of this study mentioned children's tales involving jealousy and envy: *Cinderella*, *Snow White*, and the toys from *Toy Story*. The Old Testament prophet Hosea lived out not a tale but a personal marriage tragedy when his wife Gomer prostituted herself and was sold into slavery. In jealous love, Hosea bought her back to become once more a wife faithful to him (Hos. 1–3).

Hosea's experience was a sign that showed God's people His own jealous love for them. God promised: "I will take you to be My wife forever. I will take you to be My wife in righteousness, justice, love, and compassion. I will take you to be My wife in faithfulness" (2:19-20). Here is God's holiness, justice, and jealousy all at once. And today, we who were rebels against the Holy One have been brought to Him. And because of who He is, He calls us to follow Him in these attributes.

- -

GOD'S LOVE *and Our Mission*

"To be loved of God and to be sent by God to share that love is for the Christian and the church the summum bonum, the highest and ultimate good. The inspiring words of Jesus linger still: 'So have I loved you' (John 15:9); 'So I send you' (John 20:21)."[8]

–Francis Dubose, *The Mission of God Study Bible*

Devotions

HOLY TERROR

When I was growing up, people called an out-of-control child a "holy terror." Come to find out, this phrase is still used in contemporary culture but in diverse ways. A graphic novel titled *Holy Terror* portrays a superhero named Fixer. A book with this title advocates homosexuality. A band called The Last Poets released a CD with this title in the 1990s.

None of these suggest anything remotely connected with the original concept of the holy. But the Bible is clear: There is a real God who is really, truly holy, and to encounter Him is to be filled with awe, even dread and terror. That's the way biblical characters encountered Him. At the burning bush, "Moses hid his face because he was afraid to look at God" (Ex. 3:6). When Ezekiel had a vision of Yahweh's glory, he "fell facedown" (Ezek. 1:28). The apostle John wrote, "When I saw Him, I fell at His feet like a dead man" (Rev. 1:17).

The biblical accounts in which persons come face to face with the Creator are remarkably similar. They experience that He is wholly other—not a part of the created order. Furthermore, they understand that He is holy other—separated from all taint of sin or evil. How could an encounter with Him not lead one to fear or even terror? The writer to the Hebrews confessed, "It is a terrifying thing to fall into the hands of the living God!" (Heb. 10:31).

Thus, when a human being comes face to face with God Almighty, one way to think about Him is as "The Holy Terror" in its true sense. With the ancient writer we affirm, "The fear of the LORD leads to life" (Prov. 19:23).

Pause and Reflect

1   When was the last time you experienced God's awesome presence and were filled with awe or fear?

- -

2   How would you explain to someone the positive sense of the fear of God, that is, reverence and awe?

WHEN JEALOUSY IS RIGHT

Several media superstars have publicly rejected the God of the Bible because He is jealous. This, they claim, keeps them from Christianity. Like others before them, such people have not taken into account that even in English, jealousy can have a positive as well as a negative connotation.

Sure, the Bible rightly condemns most forms of jealousy. Jealousy, in essence, is fear of losing to another something or someone that one holds dear. Thus, King Saul became jealous of David when he lost popularity after David killed Goliath (1 Sam. 18:6-9). Ten disciples became jealous of James and John when their mother asked for them to have the best seats in Jesus' kingdom (Matt. 20:20-28). Jesus rightly condemned this, counseling humble service instead.

On the other hand, we all understand proper jealousy within marriage. If I were to flirt with another woman, my wife would be jealous, and rightly so. She would also be jealous for me, her husband. What loving spouse would not be righteously jealous under such circumstances?

So our God is jealous for His human creatures. He longs for us to experience the joy and happiness we were meant to have. When we stray from Him, He wants us back. He does not want to lose us to other gods, whether the god of a false religion, the god of career and power, or the god of a relationship in which we put someone in a higher place than we put our relationship with God.

Pause and Reflect

1   Is the jealousy of a wife for her husband a good analogy for God's jealousy? Why or why not?

----

2   How confident are you that God's jealousy over you is a good thing?

----

3   Will you pray to God, thanking Him that He is a jealous God who brought you to Himself?

Imitating God's Holiness

I must confess I have made fun of "holy rollers" before. Their women looked weird, and their men were too loud. But God has convicted me for this attitude. Such people were at least taking the idea of holiness seriously. And those in a genuine relationship with God Almighty are committed to following Him in holiness—separation from sin.

Furthermore, I have learned that true holiness is like a circle: God makes us holy in conversion; we grow in personal holiness; God keeps increasing our capacity to be like Him in being separate from sin; and so on. In both Testaments, holiness is not optional:

- "Consecrate yourselves and be holy, for I am Yahweh your God. Keep My statutes and do them; I am Yahweh who sets you apart" (Lev. 20:7-8).
- "Christ loved the church and gave Himself for her to make her holy…He did this to present the church to Himself in splendor…holy and blameless" (Eph. 5:25-27).

The New Testament emphasizes that holiness comes from a transformed heart, one made new in Christ. From a new heart, the saint (or "holy one") grows in the capacity to be separate from the sins of the heart (lust, anger, greed, pride, and so on). And the pure heart then expresses itself in outwardly holy words and deeds. It was Jesus who promised, "Those who hunger and thirst for righteousness are blessed, for they will be filled" (Matt. 5:6).

Pause and Reflect

1   Do you want to imitate God in His holiness as much as you want to imitate His love? Why or why not?

- -

2   Why emphasize holiness as coming from the heart rather than as conformity to external standards?

- -

3   What heart sin (lust, anger, greed, pride, etc.) might God be leading you to separate from more intentionally?

DISCUSSION QUESTIONS

1   Is jealousy good or bad? Have you ever been a victim of someone's undeserved jealousy? What did you learn from the situation?

2   What comes to mind when you think of the word *holy*? Why do you think God is so serious about His holiness?

3   In what ways can we guard against becoming too familiar with the things of God? What is the proper response of believers in light of the holiness of God?

4   Have you ever wished that some of God's moral laws were different than they are? If so, does such a wish imply a dislike for some aspect of God's righteous character? How can we become more apt to embrace God's character and commands as always righteous and good?

5   Why should we love God for being a God of wrath who hates sin? In what ways is it right to imitate His wrath? In what ways is it wrong?

6   In what ways can we as Jesus' followers mirror God's love for and commitment to justice? What issue of justice might God be calling you to address in a more hands-on fashion?

7   How is the right jealousy of God different from the wrong jealousy of human beings? How can we reflect God's jealousy for His own honor when we hear Him dishonored in conversation or in popular culture? How can we deepen our jealousy for the honor of God's name?

8   Which of these attributes of God—holiness, justice, jealousy—do you need to wrestle with in your life right now? Why?

9   What can you do this week to reflect that you are growing in holiness because you belong to a God who is holy? What specific action can you take this week to demonstrate your commitment to justice in the world?

10   Is there inappropriate jealousy you need to confess and ask God to remove from your life? For what person in your life could you express a godly jealousy?

Part 2

GOD THE SON

God the Son, Jesus Christ, was fully divine from eternity past. And in the fullness of time, Jesus took upon Himself flesh and became fully human so as to sacrifice Himself in our place for our sins. Through His obedience, death, and resurrection, He now stands as the perfect Prophet of God who proclaims the truth, the holy Priest to represent God to man and man to God, and the righteous, promised King over all creation.

Chapter 7

Jesus' Deity

The Son of God

Voices from *the Church*

"Everything you wanted to know about God but were afraid to ask is found and embodied and expressed in Jesus...exclusively in Jesus. He alone is God, which means that no one else is." [1]

–Sam Storms

Voices from *Church History*

"You can shut Him up for a fool, you can spit at Him and kill Him as a demon; or you can fall at His feet and call Him Lord and God. But let us not come with any patronising nonsense about His being a great human teacher. He has not left that open to us. He did not intend to." [2]

–C. S. Lewis (1898-1963)

The Wizard of Oz tells the story of Dorothy Gale, a farm girl transported by tornado to the magical Oz, a land of intrigue, enchantment, and danger. Dorothy is lost—far from Kansas, far from family, far from her friends, far from all that is comfortable and known. Trapped in Oz and pursued by a wicked witch, Dorothy only wants to go home. But how? Perhaps the "wonderful wizard of Oz" can help. So she follows the yellow brick road to the Emerald City, where the wizard resides.

Unfortunately, when she arrives, she discovers the wizard to be a fraud. "Pay no attention to that man behind the curtain!" the "great and powerful Oz" says to Dorothy as Toto the dog tugs the veil and uncovers the con. The ruse is up! The wizard is not a wizard at all. He is an old charlatan, a pretender, a phony, and a fake. Relying on smoke and a machine to give the illusion of magic, the wizard professes to be great and powerful. But he is bluffing. In the end, Dorothy makes it home, but no thanks to the wizard.

Sometimes we don't realize how important it is that people actually are who they say they are. That is until we need them to do what they say they can do. Being who you claim to be is essential to being able to do what you claim you can do. Falsely claiming to be a doctor might comfort the sick until it is time to actually diagnose and cure the disease. Who wants legal or financial advice from a person merely pretending to be a lawyer or an accountant?

The same is true as we consider Jesus Christ. What if Jesus merely claimed to be God but actually wasn't? Did He even claim to be God? Who really cares if He is God? Does it even matter?

In the chapter, we will review abundant evidence for the deity of Christ while addressing the claims of those modern and ancient teachings that deny His divinity. We will also consider the implications of Christ's deity and discover that this truth is of eternal and infinite importance for the world.

Who says Jesus is God?

The testimony for Christ's deity is overwhelming. Jesus Himself, His initial disciples, His family members, His later followers, the Old Testament Scriptures, the Father, and the Holy Spirit all clearly testify to this reality. Let us hear from these "witnesses" to Jesus' deity.

Jesus Himself

Perhaps no book of the Bible presents such clear and consistent testimony of Christ's deity as the Gospel of John. From the opening verses (John 1:1-5), the Gospel presents a powerful witness to the claim that Jesus Christ is God. But no voice in this Gospel is as loud as Christ's own.

Two examples will suffice. In John 8, certain Jews accused Christ of being a demon-possessed Samaritan. Christ replied that He seeks after the glory of the Father in all things and that whoever keeps His word will never see death. The Jews responded that even the blessed patriarch Abraham died. Then, as found in John 8:56-59, the following exchange took place:

56 Your father Abraham was overjoyed that he would see My day; he saw it and rejoiced."

57 The Jews replied, "You aren't 50 years old yet, and You've seen Abraham?"

58 Jesus said to them, "I assure you: Before Abraham was, I am."

59 At that, they picked up stones to throw at Him. But Jesus was hidden and went out of the temple complex.

Even those unfamiliar with the Old Testament Scriptures can see that Christ was speaking of His eternality. The claim is even more astounding if one considers the Old Testament context: "God replied to Moses, 'I AM WHO I AM. This is what you are to say to the Israelites: I AM has sent me to you'" (Ex. 3:14). John 8:58 is perhaps the overarching "I Am" statement in the Gospel of John, yet there are others.

Let's take a look at the seven traditional "I Am" statements in the Gospel of John. To the casual reader, these might be mere coffee cup sayings. To those familiar with the Old Testament, they mean much more.

1. "**I am the bread of life**," Jesus told them. "No one who comes to Me will ever be hungry, and no one who believes in Me will ever be thirsty again" (John 6:35).
2. Then Jesus spoke to them again: "**I am the light of the world**. Anyone who follows Me will never walk in the darkness but will have the light of life" (John 8:12).
3. "**I am the door**. If anyone enters by Me, he will be saved and will come in and go out and find pasture" (John 10:9).
4. "**I am the good shepherd**. The good shepherd lays down his life for the sheep" (John 10:11).
5. Jesus said to her, "**I am the resurrection and the life**. The one who believes in Me, even if he dies, will live" (John 11:25).
6. Jesus told him, "**I am the way, the truth, and the life**. No one comes to the Father except through Me" (John 14:6).
7. "**I am the vine**; you are the branches. The one who remains in Me and I in him produces much fruit, because you can do nothing without Me" (John 15:5).

To understand the claim Jesus was making, we need to once again consider Exodus 3, where the Lord revealed His name as "I AM." By using the language "I am," Christ was doing more than simply describing Himself as preexistent. He was claiming to be Yahweh, the God of Abraham, Isaac, and Israel, the one true God. This is a radical claim with profound implications.

Or consider John 10. After claiming to be the Good Shepherd who lays down His life for His sheep (10:14-15), Christ states, "The Father and I are one" (10:30). What was the response of those who were gathered? "Again the Jews picked up rocks to stone Him" (10:31). Clearly, Jesus' claim seemed blasphemous to the Jews. Otherwise, they would not have been so offended. Jesus claimed deity for Himself.

Jesus' Disciples

Not only did Jesus testify of His deity, but so did His disciples. Perhaps no example is greater than Thomas' response to the resurrected Lord. At first skeptical, Thomas was soon won over and exclaimed, "My Lord and my God!" (John 20:28).

What would make this Jew born and bred in strict monotheism suddenly attribute deity to this Man unless he was convinced that He really was God? Bear in mind that Thomas was not merely acquainted with Christ but also one of the 12 disciples. The evidence for Christ's deity must have been overwhelmingly compelling. Even more, why would Jesus receive the worship unless it was appropriate? Again, we see that if Christ is not worthy of worship as God, then He is a blasphemous usurper of glory.

Later Apostles

Later apostles (including Jesus' own half-brother James) believed in Christ's deity. As they reflected upon the life, death, and resurrection of Christ and were inspired by the Holy Spirit, they used exalted God-honoring language for Jesus.

Consider a few examples: "The Son is the radiance of God's glory and the exact expression of His nature, sustaining all things by His powerful word. After making purification for sins, He sat down at the right hand of the Majesty on high" (Heb. 1:3). "James, a slave of God and of the Lord Jesus Christ" (Jas. 1:1). In this opening to his letter, James places Jesus on the same level as God the Father.

No chorus is as clear and crisp as Paul's chorus in Colossians 1:15-20. Read this and note all the exalted titles and descriptions given to Jesus:

15 *He is the image of the invisible God,*
the firstborn over all creation.
16 *For everything was created by Him,*
in heaven and on earth,
the visible and the invisible,

whether thrones or dominions
or rulers or authorities—
all things have been created through Him and for Him.
17 *He is before all things,*
and by Him all things hold together.
18 *He is also the head of the body, the church;*
He is the beginning, the firstborn from the dead,
so that He might come to have
first place in everything.
19 *For God was pleased to have*
all His fullness dwell in Him,
20 *and through Him to reconcile*
everything to Himself
by making peace
through the blood of His cross—
whether things on earth or things in heaven.

The Bible, God the Father, and the Holy Spirit

In addition to the testimony of Christ and His apostles, we might consider the Old Testament Scriptures (Isa. 9:6) and the witness of the Father (Matt. 3:17; 17:5) and the Holy Spirit (John 15:26). The biblical case for the deity of Christ is comprehensive.

Christ Himself, His followers and family, the Old Testament Scriptures, the Father, and the Holy Spirit all testify clearly that Jesus Christ was and is fully God. And the question Jesus put to His disciples—"Who do you say that I am?"—is the question you and I and everyone else must answer today. Will we accept that Jesus is who He says He is?

Who denies that Jesus is God?

Though orthodox Christianity has always proclaimed the deity of the Son, there have also always been false teachers who have rejected this truth. Modern denials of Christ's deity are most commonly expressed in liberalism and the many "Christian" cults.

Liberalism

According to many liberal scholars, Jesus Christ was not divine but was instead a supreme example of humanity at its greatest. For them, Christ was not Himself God but lived with an enhanced degree of God-consciousness. Jesus is thus seen as possessing vast wisdom and moral righteousness but not utter perfection.

Theological Cults

Other denials of Christ's deity, ones which many Christians are more likely to encounter, are found in the teachings of various theological cults. Though differing in exactly what they teach about the nature of Christ, both Mormons and Jehovah's Witnesses in particular share a common rejection of the deity of Christ as it is biblically presented. Christ is said to be a created being and also to be "a god" but not "the God."

When thinking about the Trinity, three words are important: *unity*, *diversity*, and *mystery*. There is a unity in the Godhead, but there is also diversity. If we emphasize unity to the neglect of diversity, we plunge off the mountain of God's revelation and tumble into an abyss of theological error. If we emphasize diversity to the neglect of divine unity, we careen off the other side into other doctrinal dangers, such as polytheism (a belief in many gods).

Both unity and diversity exist in God's tri-unity. How those truths relate is shrouded in mystery. As is often said of the Trinity, "try to understand it and you'll lose your mind; try to deny it and you'll lose your soul." This should not diminish the role of theological reflection but help us acknowledge our limits in reaching for the heights of the exalted glory of God's nature.

Why does Jesus' deity matter?

Theology is profoundly practical. As discussed in Session 1 of this study ("Knowing God and Making Him Known"), theology is not intended to be a dry and dull enterprise but rather an exciting and enriching endeavor into the very nature and works of God. What could be more beautiful and valuable than increased insight into our Creator and Redeemer?

The deity of Christ is not only exciting but also essential. There simply is no way around it. Unlike more peripheral discussions of end times or even the meaning and mode of baptism, absolutely everything unravels if we remove the thread of Christ's deity.

Why does the deity of Christ matter? The reasons are many and diverse. We will examine just a few.

1. If Christ is not divine, then the Scriptures are not true.

As we have seen, the Bible explicitly teaches that Jesus Christ is the eternal Son of God. We cannot simply reject the revelation on this point without also subjecting all of Scripture to our own whims. God's people are to subject themselves to God's Word, not subject the Word to themselves.

If the Bible is wrong on this one point, then how can God's people trust that it is not wrong on every other point? Thus, the deity of Christ is essential for our confidence in the absolute trustworthiness of God's Word. One error calls into question the truthfulness of the whole.

2. If Christ is not divine, then His sacrifice was not sufficient to save us from our sin.

The truth of Christ's deity is absolutely essential to maintain the integrity of the gospel by which we are saved. Indeed, if Christ was and is not the true God, then we are hopeless and helpless in our sins, abiding under curse and condemnation. Why is this?

In order to recognize the necessity of Christ's deity, we must understand something of the nature of sin and its due penalty. Sin is no light trespass against arbitrary, impersonal mores and laws but is instead an infinite offense against a holy King. There is no such thing as a mere misdemeanor in the kingdom of God. All sin is an assault on the glory of our Maker.

In light of this understanding of sin, the due penalty is not a slap on the wrist. An infinite offense carries an infinite debt calling for infinite punishment. But man is finite. Only an infinite being can fully and truly bear the infinite punishment that sin demands. Therefore, Jesus Christ, if truly our substitute, must have been infinite. Only God is infinite.

3. If Christ is not divine, then all glory in the work of salvation is not due to God alone.

The entirety of Scripture points to the impossibility of human beings saving themselves. As Jonah 2:9 states, "Salvation is from the LORD!" If Jesus were a mere mortal, then either He could not accomplish our salvation or the definitiveness of this statement is misleading and we share in at least some of the praise and glory for which God is jealous.

4. If Christ is not divine, then He could not represent God to man and man to God as a mediator.

There is one mediator between God and man (1 Tim. 2:5), and He is the God-man, Jesus Christ. As man, He is able to sympathize with us in our weakness and serve as our Great High Priest (Heb. 2:14-18; 4:14-16). As the eternal God, He is able to eternally intercede for and offer a final and full sacrifice on behalf of sinful people (7:22-28).

5. If Christ is not divine, then He could not reveal the image of the Father nor restore to us the image of God.

Lastly, only God can perfectly image God. While certain attributes are disclosed in creation (Rom. 1:20), created things cannot fully reveal the Creator. Therefore, in order for God to be known, God Himself must appear to His people.

Christ came to reveal the Father (John 14:8-9) and to restore in His people the image of God that was corrupted in the fall. Therefore, our greatest good is to be conformed to the image of Christ (Rom. 8:28-29), who is the "image of the invisible God" (Col. 1:15) and the "exact expression of His nature" (Heb. 1:3).

There is another reason Christ's deity is essential—the work of mission. If Christ is not divine, then we have no good news to take to the world. But if Christ is divine, then the church has a message of hope and joy and reconciliation to take to the world.

So how do we move forward on mission for Christ's kingdom? With full confidence! Because Christ is divine, we can have confidence in the authority of the Scriptures. Because Christ is divine, He has offered an infinite payment to cover our infinite debt. Because Christ is divine, salvation is fully from the Lord and all glory goes to God alone. Because Christ is divine, He is able to atone for man's sin and mediate between God and man. Because Christ is divine, we can know the Father rightly and be restored to the divine image that was once deformed.

In the work of mission, we proclaim Christ crucified—not the death of just another man but the one and only God-man, the eternal Son of God, who for us and our salvation was made man, was crucified, resurrected, and has ascended to heaven from where He will one day return.

Conclusion

Like Dorothy, we as Christians are a little out of place. This world that we know is wrought with perils. Oh, to be home! Home is more than where the heart is; it is where the Father of all lights and blessings resides. It is the fountain of all joy, life, and pleasure (Ps. 16:11). Our home is with Christ, and we await His return when He will restore all things and make them new.

Like Dorothy, we need more than the empty promises and vain illusions of a curtained charlatan. If Christ is not God, then our Christianity is empty and hopeless and we are stuck in this fallen Oz. But because He is God, our sin is forgiven. We have been reconciled to God. We have access to peace and joy. And we have a gospel to embrace and proclaim to others. The gospel and all its implications rise and fall on the deity of Christ.

Devotions

EVERYTHING FOR THE SON

Colossians 1:16: "For everything was created by Him, in heaven and on earth, the visible and the invisible, whether thrones or dominions or rulers or authorities—all things have been created through Him and for Him."

Why? The pursuit of purpose is wired into human existence. What kid does not ask why? Often to the annoyance of his or her parent, no answer is sufficient to satisfy. Each reply is merely met with another question. Layer upon layer, why follows why.

God has given us a central truth about the why behind all things. Why are trees tall and cheetahs fast? Why does the moon reflect the sun and influence the tides? Why does the earth go through distinct seasons?

Colossians 1 says that all things were created "for Him." For the glory of the Son, all things exist. But how can all things exist for Jesus Christ when the Bible is utterly clear that God will share His glory with absolutely no other? (See Isa. 42:8, for example.) How can the exclusive demands that God makes on glory be understood in light of the New Testament glorification of Christ? The biblical answer is clear—Jesus is the Christ, who is the Son of God.

Those who reject the deity of Christ do more than deny an old, dusty doctrine; they actually reject the very purpose for which they were created—to know, love, enjoy, and praise Him by whom, through whom, and for whom all things exist.

Pause and Reflect

1   What other passages in the Bible can you think of that express a truth similar to Colossians 1:16?

---

2   How does the little preposition "for" in Colossians 1:16 affect the current of the lives of those who would call themselves Christians?

---

3   How can you personally and practically apply this truth to your life?

THE FIRSTBORN

Colossians 1:18: "He is also the head of the body, the church; He is the beginning, the firstborn from the dead, so that He might come to have first place in everything."

Jacob wanted the inheritance and the blessing of his father Isaac, but what could he do? After all, Esau was the older brother (though not by much, for they were twins). As the firstborn, Esau was entitled to it all. Jacob would not be entirely overlooked, but the rights of the firstborn would never be his…unless he deceived.

This story from the Old Testament amply demonstrates the meaning of being the firstborn. The firstborn was to receive the inheritance and blessing of God passed along through the father.

In Colossians 1, the Son is referred to as the "firstborn" twice. In verse 15, He is called the "firstborn over all creation," and here in verse 18 he is the "firstborn from the dead." These passages do not imply that Christ was the first creation or the first to rise from the dead but rather that He stands supreme over all creation and over death. As verse 18 goes on to say, His firstborn status implies His preeminence ("first place in everything").

"The Father loves the Son and has given all things into His hands" (John 3:35). As the firstborn, Christ is the proper Heir to the kingdom (Gal. 3:16). However, like a good older brother, He does not keep the blessing all to Himself but instead delights to share the inheritance with those who have been adopted into the family (3:29). What wonderful news!

Pause and Reflect

1 What is the relationship between Christ's firstborn status and His preeminence?

- -

2 If Christ is the proper Heir to the blessings of the kingdom, how is it that we enter into them with Him?

- -

3 Christ is described as the head of what body? What implications does Christ's love for the church have for our interaction with brothers and sisters in Christ?

THE PRICE OF PEACE

Colossians 1:19-20: "For God was pleased to have all His fullness dwell in Him, and through Him to reconcile everything to Himself by making peace through the blood of His cross—whether things on earth or things in heaven."

"For never was a story of more woe than this of Juliet and her Romeo." The final scenes of Shakespeare's classic are breathtaking. On the cusp of drinking deeply of their adolescent love, something as insignificant as a delayed message forever parts the two.

The tale is a tragedy deep and dark, yet there is a glimmer of light toward the end as Montague and Capulet arrive. Distraught over the deaths of their beloved children, a history of hatred is put to rest there in the tomb. The blood of son and daughter has appeased the ancient feud. Hostilities cease at the beloveds' grave.

Peace comes at a price, and deeper offenses require greater costs. Mere apologies will not do as insult and injury demand a response.

No peace was more costly than that between Maker and man. Resplendent Creator and rebellious creature separated and plunged into enmity through man's sin—sin so horrifyingly tragic that the entire universe shudders in awed terror (Jer. 2:12-13). Infinite insult demanded an infinite price. What man could and would not pay, God did in the sending of His Son. The gospel is a peace-making mission. God has reconciled the rebellious through the cross and now calls us into the mission. We are ambassadors of reconciliation (2 Cor. 5:11-21). God has purchased peace and has called us to proclaim it to the world. Will we?

Pause and Reflect

1   Why do you think the sacrifice of Christ was necessary to reconcile God and man?

----

2   How do you personally and practically fulfill the role of a minister of reconciliation? What steps can you take to grow in this responsibility?

DISCUSSION QUESTIONS

1   Milli Vanilli returned their Grammy awards when it was discovered they were imposters and not the true voices in their work. Can you think of other examples of people claiming to be something they were not?

---

2   If someone who says they believe the Bible challenged your belief that Jesus is God, what passages in the Bible would you point them to?

---

3   What is the significance of the seven "I Am" statements? What does it mean for your life that He is the bread of life, the light of the world, the good shepherd, etc.?

---

4   In John 8 and 10, the Jews respond to Christ's claims by seeking to kill Him. What does this response imply about what exactly it was that Jesus was claiming?

---

5   Read slowly through Colossians 1:15-20 and note the various depictions of Christ. Additionally, consider the number of prepositions that Paul uses: Christ is over all, creation is by, through, and for Him, etc. Consider each clause and preposition, and discuss how they bolster the argument for Christ's preeminence and supremacy.

---

6   What are some attributes of God we have already covered that you see evidenced in the life and ministry of Christ? How do His works provide testimony to His deity?

---

7   What biblical passages can you think of that would provide support for the doctrine of Christ's deity?

---

8   What words would you use to describe the relationship between the Father and Son in the Godhead? Do you find the doctrine of the Trinity to be confusing, joyful, glorious, threatening, etc?

---

9   What truths would you consider absolutely essential to Christian life and doctrine? What are some doctrines that Christians can disagree on and still enjoy unity in the gospel?

---

10   What are some reasons why the deity of Christ is essential for the gospel and our salvation?

Chapter 8

Jesus' Humanity

The Son of Man

VOICES FROM *Church History*

"Man's Maker was made man, that He, Ruler of the stars, might nurse at His mother's breasts; that the Bread might be hungry, the Fountain thirst, the Light sleep, the Way be tired from the journey; that the Truth might be accused by false witnesses, the Judge of the living and the dead be judged by a mortal judge, Justice be sentenced by the unjust, the Teacher be beaten with whips, the Vine be crowned with thorns, the Foundation be suspended on wood; that Strength might be made weak, that He who makes well might be wounded, that Life might die." [1]
–Augustine (354-430)

VOICES FROM *Church History*

"A mediator is one appointed to bring together two estranged parties. He must perfectly represent both parties and do all that is necessary to bring them together. As the God-man, Jesus does this. He partakes of the nature of both God and man, and in Him they meet in reconciliation." [2]
–Herschel H. Hobbs (1907-1995)

A professor opened the class with one simple question: "What words would you use to describe humanity?" He walked to the whiteboard, dry erase marker in hand, and waited for the responses. This was a seminary class. The room was filled with pastors and theologians of tomorrow, most of whom had already studied the doctrine of humanity. Answers began to form in their minds and fly from their mouths as the professor feverishly recorded the responses on the whiteboard: Sinful. Wicked. Weak. Evil. Fallen. Needy. Broken. Idolatrous. Greedy. Lustful. Deceived. Created.

Eventually, the room grew quiet, adjectives exhausted, and the professor stepped back and stared at the words written on the board. After a long pause, he asked with a slight smirk, "These words describe humanity?"

"Yes!" the students confidently replied.

"So are you saying that these words describe Jesus or that Jesus is not human?"

Silence. The floor fell out from under the students as they scrambled to figure out just how they had fallen victim to the professor's sleight of hand.

When most of us think of humanity, we think of mankind in its current state—subject to the corruption and futility from our fall into sin; ruined and rebellious! That is the only humanity we've ever tasted and known.

But we must be careful not to apply these descriptions to humanity in general, for it hasn't always been so. In some sense, we humans haven't been fully human for quite some time. We have tasted a diluted and distorted version of humanity. People have been dehumanized by sin.

The distinction between humanity as we know it and humanity as it once was is essential if we are to rightly consider the humanity of Christ. As we will see, He identified with all that is inherent to humanity, though He Himself was sinless. He was "in all things like unto us, without sin," as the ancient creed states. Unless we distinguish original from fallen humanity, we will inadvertently obscure and blaspheme the character of Christ. He was truly and fully human. It can even be said that He was more human than you or me!

In this chapter, we will examine the evidence for the humanity of Christ and explore the various errors that reject this doctrine. The humanity of Christ means that human nature was created good, Jesus was the perfect human sacrifice for sin, and He now intercedes for us as we live for His mission in the world.

Who says Jesus is a man?

First John 1:1-4 says:

1 *What was from the beginning,*
what we have heard, what we have seen with our eyes,

what we have observed and have touched with our hands,
concerning the Word of life—
2 *that life was revealed,*
and we have seen it and we testify and declare to you
the eternal life that was with the Father
and was revealed to us—
3 *what we have seen and heard we also declare to you,*
so that you may have fellowship along with us;
and indeed our fellowship is with the Father
and with His Son Jesus Christ.
4 *We are writing these things so that our joy may be complete.*

When John wrote his first letter, he did so from personal experience. Jesus was not some transcendent principle or power, some ideal or myth, but rather flesh and blood. As one of the 12 disciples (and part of Jesus' inner circle), John was a reliable witness to the humanity of Christ. After all, this is the one who had leaned upon Christ during the last supper (John 13:23-25). According to the letter, Jesus had been seen, observed, touched, and heard.

The apostles testified to Jesus' humanity. Perhaps no summary statement captures this truth better than this: "The Word became flesh and took up residence among us. We observed His glory, the glory as the One and Only Son from the Father, full of grace and truth" (John 1:14).

But the testimony does not stop there. Not only did the apostles testify to Christ's humanity, but the Son Himself provided witness. Over 80 times in the Gospels, Jesus referred to Himself as the "Son of Man." In fact, this was His preferred way of referring to Himself. Though more can be learned from this title than a simple recognition of His humanity, certainly nothing less is implied.

Not only did Jesus claim humanity with His words, but He demonstrated it with His actions too. According to the Scriptures, Jesus experienced the following:
- He grew tired: "Jacob's well was there, and Jesus, **worn out** from His journey, sat down at the well. It was about six in the evening" (John 4:6).
- He increased in wisdom and stature: "And Jesus **increased in wisdom and stature**, and in favor with God and with people" (Luke 2:52).
- He thirsted: "After this, when Jesus knew that everything was now accomplished that the Scripture might be fulfilled, He said, 'I'm **thirsty**!'" (John 19:28).
- He grew sorrowful and troubled: "Taking along Peter and the two sons of Zebedee, He began to be **sorrowful and deeply distressed**" (Matt. 26:37); "Jesus **wept**" (John 11:35).

- He hungered: "But while they still were amazed and unbelieving because of their joy, He asked them, 'Do you have anything here to eat?' So they gave Him a piece of a broiled fish, and He took it and **ate** in their presence" (Luke 24:41-43).
- He slept: "But He was in the stern, **sleeping** on the cushion. So they woke Him up and said to Him, 'Teacher! Don't You care that we're going to die?'" (Mark 4:38).
- He even celebrated and feasted such that He was wrongly mocked as a glutton and a drunkard: "The Son of Man has come **eating and drinking**, and you say, 'Look, **a glutton and a drunkard**, a friend of tax collectors and sinners!'" (Luke 7:34).

Who denies Jesus' humanity?

First John 4:2-3 says:

> 2 *This is how you know the Spirit of God: Every spirit who confesses that Jesus Christ has come in the flesh is from God.* 3 *But every spirit who does not confess Jesus is not from God. This is the spirit of the antichrist; you have heard that he is coming, and he is already in the world now.*

In our day and age, the divinity of Christ is often under attack from false teachers who see Jesus as a good teacher but not the Son of God. Interestingly enough, one of the biggest threats the early church faced was the opposite—false teachers who denied the humanity of Christ.

What was going on culturally that made this debate so prominent? In a nutshell, Greek philosophy. Philosophers like Plato held to an understanding of the universe that saw whatever is material or physical as necessarily inferior or evil while the ideal and perfect world was purely spiritual (meaning non-material).

Nowadays, when we hear of Platonic philosophy, we're likely to think of "platonic relationships"—non-romantic, non-sexual friendships. Do you see how the notion of platonic relationships points us back to Plato's philosophy? Physical or material realities are corrupt, which means the ideal and highest form of friendship must be non-physical in nature. Take it a step further and the ideal and highest form of being must be non-physical too. In other words, the human body is something to escape from, not something worth redeeming.

This worldview infiltrated the early church as it spread through the Roman Empire. For Greeks, it seemed shameful to confess that God could have united Himself to flesh and blood. How could a perfect Being subject Himself to the lesser world of matter?

But Christianity teaches something very different. For the Christian, the universe, though presently corrupted and subjected to futility (Rom. 8:20), is not inherently evil. Rather, the material world was originally created good (Gen. 1:31). What's more, the physical resurrection of Jesus' body is proof that the world of matter matters. There are no biblical grounds for rejecting the physical world as something evil or inferior.

In addition to countering the false teachings springing from the reigning philosophies of the day, the early church sought to clarify the relationship between Christ's divine and human natures. To wrestle through the biblical testimony on this issue, a council was called at Chalcedon in 451. At that time, the orthodox understanding of the relationship between Jesus' two natures was articulated and agreed upon.

The confession set forth at Chalcedon represents the boundaries of orthodox thought on the relationship of Christ's deity and humanity. Though there is great and unfathomable mystery in regard to the incarnation, there is also clear biblical testimony as to the proper boundaries of belief. To go beyond the boundaries of the creed is to go beyond the boundaries of Scripture insofar as the creed represents a faithful summary of the Scripture, which is our final authority and arbiter on all truth.

VOICES FROM *Church History*

"Therefore, following the holy fathers, we all with one accord teach men to acknowledge one and the same Son, our Lord Jesus Christ, at once complete in Godhead and complete in manhood, truly God and truly man, consisting also of a reasonable soul and body; of one substance with the Father as regards his Godhead, and at the same time of one substance with us as regards his manhood; like us in all respects, apart from sin; as regards his Godhead, begotten of the Father before the ages, but yet as regards his manhood begotten, for us men and for our salvation, of Mary the Virgin, the God-bearer; one and the same Christ, Son, Lord, Only-begotten, recognized in two natures, without confusion, without change, without division, without separation; the distinction of natures being in no way annulled by the union, but rather the characteristics of each nature being preserved and coming together to form one person and subsistence, not as parted or separated into two persons, but one and the same Son and Only-begotten God the Word, Lord Jesus Christ; even as the prophets from earliest times spoke of him, and our Lord Jesus Christ himself taught us, and the creed of the Fathers has handed down to us."

– The Chalcedonian Creed (451)

It is important to note that the Chalcedonian definition of Christ's humanity and divinity was not "created" by the council. The doctrine was already true; it merely took some time for the church to corporately affirm the most helpfully coherent language to communicate the truth.

The early church councils (such as Chalcedon) were invaluable to the church's quest to be faithful to the Bible. They were not engaging in theology for theology's sake. They were defending the gospel. The church understood that our redemption depended on Christ's representation. If He did not fully represent humanity in its entirety, then He could not have provided a sufficient sacrifice to reconcile us to the Father.

Why does Jesus' humanity matter?

The humanity of Jesus Christ is vitally important if we are to believe the gospel. Far from a peripheral doctrine, Christ's incarnation abides at the center of the Christian confession. To compromise on His humanity is to remove an undergirding foundation of the faith. We see the utter necessity and centrality of Christ's humanity when we examine what would be lost if the doctrine were to be denied.

Christ's Obedience in Our Place

Christ is man's perfect and sufficient representative for obedience. If Christ were not fully man, He could not have obeyed fully in our place.

Romans 5:12-21 compares and contrasts two men, the first Adam—who plunged mankind into ruin—and the second Adam—who has ransomed mankind into peace. Where the first Adam rebelled and fell in the garden (Eden), the second Adam remained faithful in the garden (Gethsemane). Where Israel grumbled, mumbled, muttered, and moaned in the wilderness, Christ trusted in the Father's provision and care during His temptation in the wilderness. Christ is the new and better Adam, the new and better Man who has obeyed the Father perfectly and attained in His life the fullness of righteousness, which is credited to our account by faith.

Christ as Our Substitute Sacrifice

Christ is man's one-to-one substitute to pay for our sins. If Christ were not fully man, He could not have sacrificed Himself in our place.

Because of our sin, we all owe a debt to God. The sentence for our disobedience is clear. Death—both physical and spiritual, separation from all that is good and right, curse and condemnation—rules over man. Death loomed and boasted of its universal authority over the sons of men.

The entire Old Testament sacrificial system painted a picture. Far from being an end in itself, the daily, weekly, and yearly sacrifices under the Mosaic covenant pointed to a future sacrifice, a greater sacrifice, a final sacrifice (Heb. 10:1-14). But what could be sacrificed? It was man's sin. So man must pay. But all of us are afflicted by sin, which means we all have our own debt to pay. Only a perfectly sinless human could provide the final and full sacrifice necessary to atone for sin.

It was an infinite debt, but God is the only infinite Being. So only He could fully pay the debt. But how could God die? It sounds like a contradiction, a logical impossibility, an enigma beyond comprehension, but it's not. The Son was fully God (and thus could pay the infinite debt) and also fully man (and thus could die, ending death's reign and sin's tyranny over humanity).

Christ as Our Mediator

The death to which mankind was subjected was not merely physical but spiritual as well. We were utterly separated from God. Therefore, it was necessary that one come between us for the sake of reconciliation. We needed one who could represent God to us and us to God. Only one who was both fully and truly God and fully and truly man could do so.

If the Son were not fully human, He could not have reconciled us to the Father as our one mediator: "For there is one God and one mediator between God and humanity, Christ Jesus, Himself human" (1 Tim. 2:5).

Christ as Ruler over Creation

In the beginning, man was created in the image of God as His representative on the earth. Along with this image came the charge to rule the earth. Unfortunately, human beings forfeited this responsibility by choosing to sin. As the perfect Man, Christ has fulfilled this original intent and has been given all authority and honor (Matt. 28:18; Heb. 2:9).

If the Son were not fully human, then God's intention for a human being to rule wisely over creation would never have been fulfilled.

Christ as Our Example and Pattern in Life

The abiding hope of the Christian is his or her progressing into the likeness of Christ. Day by day we are being changed into His image (2 Cor. 3:18), and the Father is working all things in our lives toward that goal (Rom. 8:28-29).

Even now, we have an opportunity to reflect the Son of God in our lives. We do so in our suffering (1 Pet. 2:21), in our believing (Heb. 12:2), and in our walking (1 John 2:6). Furthermore, He serves as the perfect example of the "Spirit-filled" Man who lived in absolute reliance upon the Holy Spirit. We are called to model Him in this way as well. Christ serves as a perfect example and pattern toward which we seek to grow in all areas of life.

If the Son were not fully human, how could we seek to follow Him and walk as He walked?

Christ as Our High Priest

Hebrews 4:15-16 tells us that Christ is our High Priest who is able to sympathize with us in our weaknesses. That is an utterly astounding truth upon which to reflect. He was tested and tried in every way as we are, and yet He remained steadfast and sinless. Since Christ has been tested and tried as we are, He is sympathetic toward us and sits at the right hand of the Father to make intercession for us (Rom. 8:34). This should lead to great boldness as we approach the Father's throne, for we know that it is a throne of grace.

If the Son were not fully human, He could not have experienced the trials and tribulations of humanity and thus would not be sympathetic to our fragility and need.

Conclusion

The incarnation is a profound reality. One could ponder this truth for a lifetime and only scratch the surface of this mystery and beauty. And yet it is like a key to a wonderful world of complementary truths. Once the lock is turned and this door is opened, everything else fits. Without the humanity of Christ, everything else comes undone.

Marva Dawn summarizes the beauty of the incarnation this way: "Why does all this matter to me? Personally I am overwhelmed with gratitude that God should stoop so far as to become truly mortal, actually a human being, to demonstrate to us what God's 'everlasting dominion and glory and kingship' as envisioned by Daniel genuinely are and will be. I don't have to be able to explain it; I can only exclaim it: God with us, Son of Man in the flesh, reigns over the cosmos!"[3]

Devotions

A TEST OF TRUTH

The early church faced a problem. As prophesied by the apostle Paul (Acts 20:28-30), false teachers had come into Ephesus with strange twistings of the truth. The church needed a standard, a litmus test to distinguish truth from lies. It came in the form of a basic confession—"Jesus Christ has come in the flesh" (1 John 4:2).

This short phrase was not intended as a comprehensive test for orthodoxy, but it did highlight the particular false teaching facing the church at Ephesus. Furthermore, it provides for us today an abiding insight into the necessity of Christ's humanity.

The incarnation of Christ is no peripheral doctrine only relevant to ivory tower seminarians. It instead rests as a supporting pillar for the very foundations of the faith. Consider what would be lost if the Son of God were not actually a man:

• Without the incarnation, biblical truth is compromised and we cannot trust the apostolic witnesses who testified to Christ's humanity.

• Without the incarnation, Christ could not have lived a perfectly faithful life as a man and thus could not have provided a pattern for us to follow.

• Without the incarnation, Christ could not have actually died for us and thus we would still be in our sins.

In this chapter we dig into the implications of the incarnation and examine more closely why the Christian faith necessitates Christ's humanity. Any rejection of this foundational truth is an attack on the gospel itself. By this we know truth from error—by the confession of the incarnation of the Son of God.

Pause and Reflect

1   Would you be better equipped to biblically defend Christ's deity or His humanity?

- -

2   What passages might you set forth as evidence for Jesus' humanity?

- -

3   What other doctrines would be sacrificed if we were to deny Christ's humanity?

Imagining and Imaging

Spend some time reading Hebrews 2:14-18. Now consider the implications of this marvelous passage. Imagine Jesus Christ as a one year old. He hungers and cries out. He gets an ear infection and can't sleep. He is utterly helpless and humble and needy. He is totally dependent upon Joseph and Mary.

Fast forward a few years. He runs and falls down, scraping His knee and calling out for His mother. He drives a hammer into His finger and tears fill His eyes. He asks His parents "Why?" a thousand times.

This is part of what it means to imagine the radical implications of the phrase "like His brothers in every way." Pause for a second and ponder the possibilities. He cried, hungered, questioned, slept, and grew, yet without sin (4:15).

This is hard to picture. Our perspective on humanity is stained by corruption; our view is limited and obscured by a curse. The humanity we have collectively known is one that has been subjected to vanity, one that has indulged treasonous tastes for lesser things.

Christ was like us in every way, sin excluded.

Why did He unite Himself to man? That we might be reunited to the Father. What glorious news that Christ has forever participated in communion with us that we might forever commune with Him. He who was the perfect image of God bore the image of man that man might be restored to the image of God.

Pause and Reflect

1   What reasons are given in Hebrews 2:14-18 for Christ's incarnation?

- -

2   How does the fact that Christ was tested and suffered provide assurance that He will help "His brothers" in their own suffering?

The Humiliation of Humanity

Take a few moments to read Philippians 2:5-8. Now think back to the Old Testament account of Nebuchadnezzar, the king who stood on the roof of his palace and gazed at the glory and beauty of Babylon. "All of this I have done for my majesty" he boasted. Suddenly a voice boomed and the king was driven from the palace to the fields. The ruler became a beast (Dan. 4:28-33).

Nebuchadnezzar's humiliation is in satirical contrast to the incarnation of Jesus Christ. Nebuchadnezzar, a man, sought his own glory and was humbled by becoming like a beast. Christ, the King of all creation, humbled Himself by becoming a man that He might be exalted as the Ruler of all. The irony is thick. All the glory of mankind, all of our trinkets and treasures, all in which we boast, all is shameful compared to the glory of God.

In love, Christ humbled Himself for us by becoming like us that we might become like Him. Paul's command is clear—"become like Him in this humility." This means a death to self, death to preference, death to rights and privileges. It means that the mission of the renown of the King and His kingdom has become more important than our honor and inclinations.

What is the mission? We exist to glorify God by making disciples through the proclamation and display of the gospel. May our lives exist to that end. Christ poured Himself into humanity that we might pour ourselves out for His name.

Pause and Reflect

1   How does the incarnation of Christ compel us to live missionally?

----

2   What does it look like for you to live missionally? How do you pursue that on a practical level?

----

3   What changes do you need to make to live more strategically for the King and His kingdom?

DISCUSSION QUESTIONS

1   When asked to describe humanity, why do people immediately think of humanity in its fallen state? Why is it important to think of humanity in light of Jesus?

2   What do you think of this quote from J. I. Packer: "But in fact the real difficulty, the supreme mystery with which the gospel confronts us...lies not in the Good Friday message of atonement, nor in the Easter message of resurrection, but in the Christmas message of Incarnation." [4] Without diminishing the beauty and glory of the atonement or resurrection, how can you increase your appreciation for the incarnation?

3   Consider the various implications of Christ being fully human. Can you imagine Him with a stomach virus or stubbing His toe? What common human experiences would He share? If it is difficult for you to think of Jesus sharing common human experiences with us, what does this say about your view of Christ's humanity?

4   In what ways does the belief that physical matter is bad play out in our society? Are there ways that Christians unintentionally downplay or denigrate the value of the human body?

5   What if Christ were only partly human? How would that have restricted the redemption He provided?

6   What doctrines might be sacrificed if we were to compromise on the truth of Christ's humanity? How does every other aspect of the gospel unravel if we lose this doctrine?

7   How do you feel about the concept of early church creeds? What is logically inconsistent with a phrase such as "No creed but the Bible"?

8   How does the truth of Christ as our mediator bring you hope and comfort? How does this relate to the way we pray (to the Father, in Jesus' name)?

9   How does the truth that Jesus faced and overcame temptation offer you hope in the middle of your own temptations and trials?

Chapter 9

Jesus' Work

Prophet, Priest, and King

Voices from *Church History*

"I believe that Jesus of Nazareth was the Saviour of the world, the Messiah so long foretold: That being anointed with the Holy Ghost, he was a Prophet, revealing to us the whole will of God: That he was a Priest, who gave himself a sacrifice for sin, and still makes intercession for transgressors: That he is a King, who has power in heaven and in earth, and will reign till he has subdued all things to himself." [1]

–John Wesley (1703-1791)

Voices from *Church History*

"For this cause…He took on Him our flesh, only for Love to man, that He might have mercy upon us…For He saw us, cast on the ground, perishing, tyrannized over by Death, and He had compassion on us." [2]

–John Chrysostom (circa 347-407)

Have you ever asked someone what their parents or spouse do for a living and found they didn't know the answer? Probably not. Unless your loved one works for the CIA, how can you not know what they do vocationally?

Now think about what happens when you meet someone for the first time. After the exchange of names, what tends to be the first question? It's usually "What do you do for a living?"

Vocation is more than a circumstantial element of our lives. What we do often says a lot about who we are. So it is with the Son of God. Christ's vocation—His occupation, His calling—was to glorify the Father and accomplish the work that He had appointed Him to do (John 4:34). This was accomplished in every single teaching and task. Not a minute of a day went by that the Son was not doing the work of the Father.

When we want to get to know a person, we ask what they do. If we would seek to know the Son of God, we should avail ourselves of the opportunity to consider who He is through the lens of what He has accomplished.

To fully appreciate the work of the Son of God, we must begin in the Old Testament for some background context and foreshadowing. There we find three particular offices ordained for the nation of Israel: prophet, priest, and king. The prophet spoke the words of God to His people. The priest offered sacrifices and prayers on behalf of the people. The king reigned over and on behalf of God's people.

To be ordained to each office, a person was anointed with oil (prophet: 1 Kings 19:16; priest: Ex. 29:1-30; king: 1 Sam. 16:6-13) and set apart to accomplish his respective role among and on behalf of the people. Each office functioned in some manner to mediate between the Lord and His people.

The most popular title used of Jesus is "Christ." This term comes from the Greek word *Christos,* which represents the Jewish hope of a coming Messiah. Both *Christ* and *Messiah* mean "anointed one."

In this chapter, we will focus our study on the particular roles (or offices) that Jesus Christ fulfilled: prophet, priest, and king. In fulfilling these roles, He thus fulfilled three functions: revelation, reconciliation, and reign. Likewise, we will see that we are subsequently called to be prophets, priests, and kings. Our ministry in the world is to reflect the ministry of Christ.

Jesus is the Prophet who reveals God to us (Acts 3:22-26).

22 *Moses said:*

The Lord your God will raise up for you a Prophet like me from among your brothers. You must listen to Him in everything He will say to you. 23 *And everyone who will not listen to that Prophet will be completely cut off from the people.*

24 *In addition, all the prophets who have spoken, from Samuel and those after him, have also announced these days.* 25 *You are the sons of the prophets and of the covenant that God made with your ancestors, saying to Abraham, And all the families of the earth will be blessed through your offspring.* 26 *God raised up His Servant and sent Him first to you to bless you by turning each of you from your evil ways.*"

Many times, the thought of Old Testament prophets conjures up powerful images and stories. Who can forget the accounts of Jonah and the fish, Daniel and the lion's den, or Hosea and his wife? Throughout the Old Testament we find pictures of God's providence and power displayed through His prophets. And we see how they delivered God's message and called people to faith and repentance.

No prophet boasted a greater authority than Moses. He spoke to God face to face as with a friend (Ex. 33:11) and not in riddles (Num. 12:8). Moses' authority as a prophet was unique and glorious (Heb. 3:1-6), yet he himself prophesied of another who would come after him with an authority greater than his own. Beyond his general prophecy of many prophets to speak God's words to the people, Moses hinted toward the coming of one Prophet in particular.

In the passage above, the apostle Peter made it clear. The prophet whom Moses pointed to was none other than Jesus Himself, the Son of God. Jesus is the greater Prophet who has come into the world. But He is unlike those who have gone before in the office. He does not merely speak the words of God, He is the Word of God. He does not merely speak the truth, He is the truth. He not only gives us God's revelation, He is God's revelation.

"The Word became flesh and took up residence among us," wrote the apostle John. "We observed His glory, the glory as the One and Only Son from the Father, full of grace and truth" (John 1:14).

Jesus said this about Himself: "I am the way, the truth, and the life. No one comes to the Father except through Me" (John 14:6).

And the writer to the Hebrews showed how God has spoken to us by sending His Son: "Long ago God spoke to the fathers by the prophets at different times and in different ways. In these last days, He has spoken to us by His Son. God has appointed Him heir of all things and made the universe through Him" (Heb. 1:1-2).

Christ is not merely the messenger but indeed the message. As prophet, Christ reveals Himself, the truth and Word of God. The good news of the Son's life, death, resurrection, and future return is the revelation of God's plan and power for redemption.

Christians as Prophets

As Christians, we are called to mirror Christ's prophetic role to the world. Through our faithful witness to the gospel, we will speak boldly and graciously about sin and our need for a Savior. We will speak out against injustice and point people to the one true Judge. Just as the Old Testament prophets called people to repentance, we must be faithful to call people to repent and trust in Jesus—the Prophet who reveals God to us. By proclaiming the gospel with our words and demonstrating the gospel with our actions, we fulfill our role as salt and light in the world (Matt. 5:13-16).

Jesus is the Priest who reconciles us to God (Heb. 2:14-18).

14 *Now since the children have flesh and blood in common, Jesus also shared in these, so that through His death He might destroy the one holding the power of death—that is, the Devil—* 15 *and free those who were held in slavery all their lives by the fear of death.* 16 *For it is clear that He does not reach out to help angels, but to help Abraham's offspring.* 17 *Therefore, He had to be like His brothers in every way, so that He could become a merciful and faithful high priest in service to God, to make propitiation for the sins of the people.* 18 *For since He Himself was tested and has suffered, He is able to help those who are tested.*

You know that feeling at the end of the day when you realize how much work you never got around to finishing? I would imagine the life of a priest in the Old Testament felt the same. The work of the priest was never finished.

The primary responsibility of a priest was to make sacrifices on behalf of the people. The problem with this system was that the blood of bulls and goats could never suffice to atone for sin (Heb. 10:4). Furthermore, the priests themselves were sinful. The work of the priest was never complete. Another day, another sacrifice, yet never full atonement. The cycle was never-ending.

The futility of the endless sacrifices in the Old Testament pointed forward to the coming of a better Priest, one who would offer up a better sacrifice. This Priest would truly and fully atone for sin. Jesus Christ, the Son of God, is the fulfillment of the Old Testament priesthood:

- Whereas the former priestly ministry was temporal, the ministry of Christ is eternal: "Now many have become Levitical priests, since they are prevented by death from remaining in office. But because He remains forever, He holds His priesthood permanently. Therefore, He is always able to save those who come to God through Him, since He always lives to intercede for them" (Heb. 7:23-25).

- Whereas the blood of bulls and goats could never atone for sin, the blood of Christ was sufficient: "For it is impossible for the blood of bulls and goats to take away sins…By this will of God, we have been sanctified through the offering of the body of Jesus Christ once and for all" (Heb. 10:4,10).

- Whereas the Levitical priests stood daily to signify that their work was never complete, Christ sat down at the right hand of the Father: "Every priest stands day after day ministering and offering the same sacrifices time after time, which can never take away sins. But this man, after offering one sacrifice for sins forever, sat down at the right hand of God" (Heb. 10:11-12).

- Whereas sacrifices were offered daily, Christ has offered one final and full offering: "For by one offering He has perfected forever those who are sanctified" (Heb. 10:14).

Christ's sacrifice implies a number of things, but among them are the truths of His deity and humanity. In order to be sacrificed in the first place, Christ must have been human (just as we saw in the previous session). In order for the sacrifice to be sufficient to cover sin, Christ must have been perfect and unblemished, thus implying deity (as we saw two sessions ago).

As Christ is the Priest who can enter into the holy of holies through His perfect and sufficient sacrifice (4:14), He is able to make intercession for His people (7:25).

Christians as Priests

As we are called to image Christ in His prophetic role, so we as Christians are called to mirror Him in His priestly role. The Bible calls us a royal and holy priesthood (1 Pet. 2:5,9). Obviously, we do not function as priests by offering ourselves as atoning sacrifices but rather by carrying out two duties: reconciliation and intercession.

As priests, we are called to highlight for the people of God the sacrifice that was offered before Him. As the Levitical priests would lift up the sacrifice of a beast for all to see, so we lift up the gospel and proclaim the sufficiency of Christ for a lost and dying world. In this sense, our role as priests mirrors our call to a life of mission.

Additionally, as Christ interceded for the people in His role as priest, so we are called to a life of intercession for the world. We pray for others, weep for their salvation, and run with arms outstretched to the places where humans need God's merciful response.

Jesus is the King who reigns over all (Rev. 19:11-16).

11 *Then I saw heaven opened, and there was a white horse. Its rider is called Faithful and True, and He judges and makes war in righteousness. 12 His eyes were like a fiery flame, and many crowns were on His head. He had a name written that no one knows except Himself. 13 He wore a robe stained with blood, and His name is the Word of God. 14 The armies that were in heaven followed Him on white horses, wearing pure white linen. 15 A sharp sword came from His mouth, so that He might strike the nations with it. He will shepherd them with an iron scepter. He will also trample the winepress of the fierce anger of God, the Almighty. 16 And He has a name written on His robe and on His thigh: KING OF KINGS AND LORD OF LORDS.*

In the Old Testament, God ruled over the people as the King of Israel, but His reign was not sufficient in the hearts of the people. They wanted to be like the other nations (1 Sam. 8:5). God warned them that kings would oppress the people and ultimately lead them astray, but He granted their request and raised up various kings to rule over the people.

One by one the kings failed. Even the faithful and good rulers such as David, Solomon, Hezekiah, and Josiah were frail and fallen leaders. But there was always a golden thread woven through the Old Testament pointing forward to a coming King who would reign in perfect peace and righteousness.

- "For a child will be born for us, a son will be given to us, and the government will be on His shoulders. He will be named Wonderful Counselor, Mighty God, Eternal Father, Prince of Peace. The dominion will be vast, and its prosperity will never end. He will reign on the throne of David and over his kingdom, to establish and sustain it with justice and righteousness from now on and forever. The zeal of the LORD of Hosts will accomplish this" (Isa. 9:6-7).

- " 'The days are coming'—this is the Lord's declaration—'when I will raise up a Righteous Branch of David. He will reign wisely as king and administer justice and righteousness in the land" (Jer. 23:5).

This king has come, and He is Jesus the Christ, the Son of God.

Jesus Christ taught constantly about the kingdom of God. Just read the Sermon on the Mount and the various parables collected in the Gospels and you'll see the emphasis the Lord placed upon the truth of the kingdom.

In some sense, the kingdom has *already come*. The Bible speaks of the rule and reign of Christ in the hearts of His people as a present reality (Matt. 4:17; 12:28). His rule is evidenced in numerous ways, but one of the clearest testimonies is in His resurrection and ascension to the right hand of the Father (Acts 2:22-36).

Though the Son reigns now, in another sense we might note that the kingdom is *yet to come*. That's why we're instructed to pray to that end (Matt. 6:10). In this understanding, the rule and reign of Christ will be evidenced when He returns and suppresses all His enemies, destroys death, and judges the world (1 Cor. 15:24-28).

This recognition of the present and yet coming perspectives of the kingdom is typically referred to as "the already and the not yet." Christ already rules and reigns as King, but that kingdom has not yet been fully established. Positions on the degrees of the present reign in contrast to the future reign differ among theologians, but most recognize the kingdom's present and future reality.

Christians as Kings

As with Christ's prophetic and priestly roles, so Christians share in His reign (Rev. 22:5). Though the shared reign of believers with Christ is clearly attested in Scripture, the form of that reign is shrouded in mystery.

There is a vast array of glorious implications of Christ's kingship. The church will surely overcome (Matt. 16:18); we will live forever, for death will be destroyed (1 Cor. 15:26); all injustice and sorrow will be wiped away eternally (Rev. 21:1-4). Indeed, all things will be made new (21:5).

But the implications are not reserved for the end of time. Indeed even now, the reign and rule of Christ should affect our daily lives in various ways. One of the most profound implications of Christ's reign is the certainty of the accomplishment of His great commission (Matt. 28:18-20).

The reign and rule of Christ even today at the right hand of the Father should give the church great confidence in the work with which we have been entrusted. All authority has been granted to the Son. So when we go and proclaim the gospel, we do so in His authority and with the help of the Holy Spirit.

Conclusion

"What do you do?" This is not merely a cultural icebreaker. It is a question packed with meaning and insight. A person's vocation can often tell us quite a bit about that person. So it is with Christ.

The Son of God is the greater Moses, the Prophet who mediates the Word of God to us. The Son of God is the greater High Priest, who offered Himself as a propitiation for our sins and now lives to make intercession for His people. The Son of God is the greater David, the King who reigns and rules in perfect righteousness.

As Prophet, Priest, and King, we are assured that Jesus loves us, intercedes for us, has reconciled us to God, and will surely keep us to the end. What glorious truths!

As the Christ, the Anointed One, Jesus has perfectly fulfilled the threefold offices of the Old Testament. As those who have been anointed by the Spirit (1 John 2:27), we too are anointed for the work of mission and are to pour ourselves out as prophets, priests, and kings on behalf of the church and a lost world.

- -

VOICES FROM *Church History*

"Praise Him! praise Him! Jesus, our blessed Redeemer!
Sing, O earth, His wonderful love proclaim!
Hail Him! hail Him! highest archangels in glory,
Strength and honor give to His holy name!
Like a shepherd, Jesus will guard His children;
In His arms He carries them all day long.

Praise Him! praise Him! Jesus, our blessed Redeemer!
Heav'nly portals loud with hosannas ring!
Jesus, Savior, reigneth forever and ever;
Crown Him! crown Him! Prophet and Priest and King!
Christ is coming, over the world victorious;
Power and glory unto the Lord belong!

Praise Him! praise Him! tell of His excellent greatness!
Praise Him! praise Him! ever in joyful song!"
–Fanny J. Crosby (1820-1915)

Devotions

THE KING SPEAKS

Hebrews 1:1-2: "Long ago God spoke to the fathers by the prophets at different times and in different ways. In these last days, He has spoken to us by His Son. God has appointed Him heir of all things and made the universe through Him."

On August 15, 1945, the Japanese emperor spoke. In the historic "Jewel Voice Broadcast," Emperor Hirohito declared that Japan had accepted the Potsdam Declaration. Not only was this message memorable for the official cessation of WWII hostilities but also because it was the first time ever for the common people of Japan to hear the voice of their ruler.

The people of Japan had heard various officials declare the words of the emperor, but there was something distinct about hearing him firsthand. There is something significant about direct speech.

God had been speaking to His people for thousands of years through the prophets. These words were true and authoritative. Furthermore, He had preserved His Word from corruption in the sacred Scriptures. God's people had heard Him speak through various prophets at various times.

Yet there is something distinct about the way that He has spoken through His Son. Christ is a prophet, but He is more. For He is not merely the messenger but is also the message. The incarnation and teaching of Christ are woven together with His crucifixion, resurrection, and ascension to proclaim news more glorious and final than that spoken before. The messenger and the message are inseparable for Christ has died, Christ has risen, and Christ will come again.

Pause and Reflect

1 What is distinctive about the message and ministry of Christ from all previous prophets?

----

2 How can you posture yourself to better hear the Son speak? What practical steps will you take today to listen?

DINING WITH ROYALTY

Imagine visiting Great Britain and receiving an invitation to dine with the royal family. Consider it from two different scenarios involving how that invitation was extended. In the first, unbelievable as it may be, you happen upon the crown prince and he personally invites you to dinner. In the second, you are simply touring the city and your cab driver tells you that he knows a guy who knows a guy who can get you in. In which of these scenarios do you have confidence that you will actually and safely enter Buckingham Palace?

Take a moment to read Hebrews 4:14-16. One of the aspects of Christ's work that we consider in this chapter is His priestly office. Now the priesthood of Christ is distinct from the priesthood of the Old Testament in a number of ways. One of the more significant truths highlighted in this text and the ensuing discussion is the fact that Christ was Himself directly appointed by the Father (5:5-6).

The fact that Christ Himself, God in the flesh, has offered us access to the throne of grace should instill confidence and boldness. Grace is not merely extended from another sinner who himself is unworthy to enter in, like the cab driver, but is instead offered from the very Son of the throne, One who has the right and authority to extend such an invitation.

Christ is our High Priest. As both the One who offers the sacrifice and is Himself the sacrificial offering, Christ has secured access for us to approach the Father.

Pause and Reflect

1   How does the gospel message of Christ's death and resurrection relate to our confidence to approach God's throne?

---

2   How does this truth play out in your life personally? Do you approach the throne with arrogant presumption or fearful timidity or do you draw near with humble boldness?

REIGN AND REDEMPTION

Revelation 7:9-10: "After this I looked, and there was a vast multitude from every nation, tribe, people, and language, which no one could number, standing before the throne and before the Lamb. They were robed in white with palm branches in their hands. And they cried out in a loud voice: Salvation belongs to our God, who is seated on the throne, and to the Lamb!"

Close your eyes and try to picture this scene. How large is the "vast multitude"? How loud were the cries? Can you see the people, the throne, the Lamb and robes and branches?

Imagine what it is like for peoples of every nation, tongue, and tribe to gather together. No jostling for position or riots, but rather a global community of shared delight. And where are they gathered? Around the throne.

There exists an inseparable bond between the kingship of Christ and the work of mission. The reign of Christ empowers evangelism, for it gives the church confidence that His mission will be accomplished. His authority bolsters our assurance that He will indeed be praised by every tongue, tribe, and nation. Without confidence in the power and love of God, mission suffers, for its biblical fuel has been drained.

This scene of a vast multitude gathered around the throne is not fanciful, wishful thinking but is a reality that will be realized. And it will occur through the words and blood of the church as we take the gospel to the ends of the earth. As we go about the work of reconciliation, let us do so with assurance of Christ's authority. His reign is the foundation upon which we carry forth the message of His redemption.

Pause and Reflect

1   Why is it important that we recognize that the work of mission is dependent upon the reign of Christ? What false inferences can we draw from this dependence?

- -

2   How is God more glorified in the expansion of the gospel to global proportions?

DISCUSSION QUESTIONS

1   In your own words, answer the question "What did the Son of God do?" How many different ways can you think of to properly answer that question?

2   How does Jesus as an "Anointed One" parallel the various offices of prophet, priest, and king? What historical event in the life of Jesus from the Gospels evidences a particular time of anointing?

3   What Old Testament stories come to mind when you think about prophets? How many prophets can you name?

4   How can you practically pursue greater faithfulness to your calling to a prophetic role within your community? Are there currently areas of your life where you are unable to see how the gospel applies? Or areas in which you are hesitant to proclaim the power of the gospel?

5   What comes to mind when you hear the word *priest*? What was the role of a priest within the Old Testament?

6   What are the implications of truly believing that Christ's one offering of Himself was sufficient to completely cover and cleanse us? How should this reality affect the way you live your life?

7   Read Hebrews 4:14; 7:25; 10:19-25. What are the specified benefits of Christ's work? What should be our response?

8   Do you struggle with thinking of God as angry toward sin and sinners? Do you struggle with believing that He is pleased with you on account of Christ? How does Jesus' high priestly role help with these struggles?

9   What images do you see when you think of royalty? How might our conceptions of royalty influenced by modern pictures (such as Great Britain's monarchy) adversely affect our understanding of Christ as King? Are there any positive correlations?

10   How can you increase your confidence in the authority and power of Christ? What are the implications of full confidence in the authority and power of Christ for how you live on mission for His kingdom?

Part 3

GOD THE SPIRIT

God the Spirit, the third Person of the Trinity, was promised by Jesus to indwell believers. He acts in the world to reveal the reality of sin and the hope of our Savior. He purifies from sin and empowers believers with gifts and fruit so that the body of Christ, the church, might be built up and sent on mission into the world to proclaim the wondrous glories of "The God Who Is" that even more might believe and worship Him.

Chapter 10

The Spirit's Identity

The Person of the Holy Spirit

VOICES FROM *Church History*

"The Holy Spirit, without whom we can neither love God nor keep His commandments."[1]
–Augustine (354-430)

VOICES FROM *the Church*

"The church becomes irrelevant when it becomes purely a human creation. We are not all we were made to be when everything in our lives and churches can be explained apart from the work and presence of the Spirit of God."[2]
–Francis Chan

While packing up their house for a move, a coworker and his wife found their 26-year-old daughter's high school diaries. With her permission, they read through them over the course of several weeks. Chuckling over the contents, the father said, "Apparently, we weren't the perfect parents we thought we were!"

In reading the diaries and discussing them with their daughter, this man and his wife gained new insights into their relationship. They learned things they had never known before. They already had a solid relationship with their daughter, but the written records of her thoughts took them deeper into her mind-set and helped them know their daughter even better.

The best interpreter of any book is the author. When it comes to the Bible, we understand the Scriptures as we submit to the guidance of the same Spirit who inspired the authors. The Scriptures not only shine light on who the Holy Spirit is, the Holy Spirit Himself shines light on what God's Word says about Himself. In other words, we learn about the Holy Spirit by reading about Him and by encountering Him as He illuminates our reading.

In this chapter, we will see that the Holy Spirit is God's great gift to the believing community. The Bible teaches that the Spirit is a Person with a distinct mission from the Father and the Son. The Bible also teaches that the Spirit is God. Because of the Holy Spirit's presence and work, we are able to have a relationship with God and join Him on His mission to seek and save the lost.

The Holy Spirit is a Person whose presence was promised by Jesus (John 14:16-17).

Too often Christians neglect the Holy Spirit. We think of His work as being relegated to the emotional or mysterious aspects of the Christian life. We know less about God the Spirit than God the Father and God the Son, and so we don't give Him as much attention.

But the Bible reveals the Holy Spirit to be an equal, essential, and personal member of the Trinity. In John 14:16-17, the Spirit is promised by Jesus to the disciples as the One who will guide, comfort, and empower them after Jesus' resurrection. Take a look:

16 *And I will ask the Father, and He will give you another Counselor to be with you forever.* 17 *He is the Spirit of truth. The world is unable to receive Him because it doesn't see Him or know Him. But you do know Him, because He remains with you and will be in you.*

Jesus promised the Spirit was coming. On the night He was betrayed, as His disciples feared the future, Jesus promised to send the Counselor—the Spirit of truth. Not just a force. Not just a power. Jesus promised to send a Person.

Does this mean the Spirit wasn't already present in the scriptural story line? Not at all. We can see the Holy Spirit at work in the Old Testament. He was active at the moment of creation, where He is described as "hovering" over the waters (Gen. 1:2), in the way a bird hovers or watches over its young. Later we see the Spirit involved in gifting people for specific tasks and anointing the ministry of important people God used (Ex. 35:30-31; 1 Sam. 16:13).

As the story line of the Bible unfolds, it becomes clearer who the Holy Spirit is. The New Testament describes Him as a Person, not just a presence. Even the biblical authors' use of pronouns to describe the Holy Spirit reinforces His personhood. If we lose sight of the truth that the Holy Spirit is a Person, we will fail to depend on Him the way we should.

In my extended family, there is a husband and wife who got married after a short courtship. After the ceremony, the groom's mother wept and lamented the new addition to the family—her daughter-in-law. For years and years until she died, the mother pestered the couple and sought to destroy their marriage, belittling her daughter-in-law at family gatherings and behaving horribly toward her. Even now, my family members shake their heads at the past antics of this woman, and the daughter-in-law still remembers how her husband's mother would refer to her as "that thing my son married." Sadly, there was never any reconciliation due to the mother's insistence on seeing her daughter-in-law as a "thing," not a person.

If we are to have a proper view of the Holy Spirit, we ought to take care to think of Him, speak of Him, and have a relationship with Him as a Person. The Holy Spirit is not an impersonal force. He is not a "thing." When we accidentally speak of the Spirit and use the pronoun "it" rather than "He," we are betraying a fundamental misunderstanding about His personhood. Jesus promised to send us a Counselor—the Spirit of truth, not merely a nebulous presence. He is our Helper, our Comforter, and our Advocate. These are words that describe a Person.

We can see in the Scriptures that the Holy Spirit is a Person, not just because of the titles given to Him but also the actions attributed to Him. The Holy Spirit can be grieved (Eph. 4:30). He can be quenched (1 Thess. 5:19). He can be resisted (Acts 7:51). It's hard to imagine a power being grieved, isn't it?

That's why we must remember the Spirit is a Person. Whenever God's children are in the midst of gossip, hate, unkindness, bitterness, or a family feud, the Spirit of God is grieved. The Holy Spirit can be saddened by our behavior.

This kind of talk only makes sense if we are thinking of the Spirit in terms of relationship. The Holy Spirit responds to our behavior. As believers in Christ, our relationship with God is made possible by the Holy Spirit. He lives in us. This means that we are relating to the Holy Spirit whether we are conscious of this relationship or not. By telling us not to grieve or quench the Spirit, the apostle Paul was implying that there are actions we can take that limit the Spirit's work in our lives and the impact God desires to have through us.

It's funny sometimes to watch people on television who want to renovate their homes. They listen politely to the advice of an expert designer and then proceed to completely ignore the counsel. Because they have nurtured their own ideas for so long, they reject time-tested wisdom. Inevitably, the renovation takes too long, they go over budget, they realize the expert was right, and they find it takes them months longer than expected to sell the house. This plot line makes for interesting television. Unfortunately, it's often the way some Christians choose to live the Christian life.

The Holy Spirit is in the "renovation" business. God the Spirit is the One who is making us new. He is the One who is forming us into the image of Christ. When we try to stay in charge of our own renovation by making compromises, the process of our transformation is slowed.

The Holy Spirit is God (2 Cor. 13:13).

It is bad enough to minimize the personhood of the Holy Spirit. But even worse, when we ignore the Spirit, we are actually ignoring God. The New Testament not only teaches that the Spirit is a Person, it also teaches that the Spirit is God. If we focus only on God the Father and God the Son while minimizing God the Spirit, we are failing to be thoroughly trinitarian.

But how do we know the Holy Spirit is God? Take a look at the way the apostle Paul closed his second Letter to the Corinthians:

13 *The grace of the Lord Jesus Christ, and the love of God, and the fellowship of the Holy Spirit be with all of you.*

Right there we see all three Persons of the Trinity: the grace of *Christ*, the love of *God*, and the fellowship of the *Spirit*—three Persons. But how do we know this Spirit with whom we have fellowship is equal with God Himself?

The Spirit is referenced interchangeably with God in several places in the New Testament. Consider Acts 5:1-11, where we read about Ananias and Sapphira. This couple sold a piece of property and deceptively kept back some of the profit while saying they were giving it all to the church. Peter confronted them by pointing out how they had lied to "the Holy Spirit." Then when he repeated the accusation, Peter referenced God in place of the Holy Spirit: "You have not lied to men but to God!"

Likewise, certain attributes that belong to God alone are ascribed to the Spirit. An example is the Spirit being described as eternal when only God is eternal (Heb. 9:14).

Understanding the truth that the Holy Spirit is God is not important just so we can win a debate with people who disagree. The beauty is that only this truth makes it possible for God to truly be with us today. The Bible is clear: It is the Holy Spirit who is living in us. We are God's tabernacle.

In the Old Testament, we read about the tabernacle as a portable sacred tent where God met with His people (Ex. 33:7-10). The Hebrew term *mishkan*, translated "tabernacle," means "dwelling place." The first tabernacle, or "tent of meeting," was built because of the sin of the Israel when they worshiped the golden calf. It was the place where God came to dwell in their midst.

When Solomon built the first temple (patterned after the tabernacle), it was built because of God's desire to be present with His people. The temple represented the presence of God.

But today, on this side of the cross and resurrection (and Pentecost!), we are God's dwelling place. In 1 Corinthians 3:16-17, Paul described believers as God's sanctuary: "Don't you yourselves know that you are God's sanctuary and that the Spirit of God lives in you? If anyone destroys God's sanctuary, God will destroy him; for God's sanctuary is holy, and that is what you are." As Sinclair Ferguson describes it, "the Spirit's coming inaugurates a communion with Christ in which the Spirit who dwelt on Christ now dwells on and in believers."[3] Isn't this good news? The beauty of the gospel is that because of Christ's death and resurrection, God dwells in us by His Spirit!

The Holy Spirit matters.

This has been a lesson full of doctrinal truths. Some may wonder what all this has to do with the Christian life. Why is it important that we understand the Holy Spirit is a Person and that He is equal with God?

The Holy Spirit makes possible our relationship with God.

These doctrinal truths matter because it is the Holy Spirit who makes our relationship with God possible. Our relationship with God, our worship, our transformation, and our good deeds are all dependent upon the Holy Spirit. There is no Christian life without Him. We are deceived if we think we can love, obey, or worship Jesus without the presence or the power of the Holy Spirit. Consider Romans 8:9-10: "You, however, are not in the flesh, but in the Spirit, since the Spirit of God lives in you. But if anyone does not have the Spirit of Christ, he does not belong to Him. Now if Christ is in you, the body is dead because of sin, but the Spirit is life because of righteousness."

To know any truth about God, we must learn it through the Holy Spirit because He is God. Anything good we do for God is done through the power of the Holy Spirit. He matters. From His work of regeneration, to His indwelling presence, to His empowering our obedience, and His setting us free from sin—our new lives in Christ are made possible because of the promised Spirit.

The Holy Spirit assures us of the closeness of God.

Likewise, the Holy Spirit matters because His presence assures us of the closeness of God. God is not a distant and faraway Deity. He is up close and personal.

Turn back to the passage we looked at earlier: John 14:16-17. When Jesus promised His disciples that He would send the Holy Spirit, He made it clear that the Spirit would provide and care for them. He was giving them the assurance that another Comforter would come. In other words, the Spirit is just like Jesus. He is God.

Francis Chan asks an important question: "Have you ever thought about the significance of having 'another' Counselor who is 'just like' Christ?" What an amazing promise! But then he continues with this challenge: "Those of us who believe in Jesus would never deny the truth that we have the Spirit of the living God, the Spirit of Him who raised Jesus from the dead, living inside of us. I'm just not convinced we've internalized this truth and enjoyed His blessings as He intends. It seems like this is mostly head knowledge to us, and that we have not owned it. It has not really made much of a difference in our lives, to the degree that if we woke up tomorrow and discovered that it is not true the Holy Spirit lives inside of us, most likely our lives wouldn't look much different." [4]

The Holy Spirit empowers us as we fulfill God's mission.

"A chain is only as strong as its weakest link." If you've ever felt like you're one of the "stronger" links, you probably don't like the truth of this proverb. I recall one day during our high school band rehearsal when it seemed we had more weak links than usual. We were preparing for concert competition, and the music was not coming together at all. Our band director's frustration was reaching an all-time high when he suddenly threw down his baton and declared, "We have a unique problem here, folks. We have some superstars and individual achievers who are so focused on their own success and recognition that we can't come together as a group."

To say I was stunned would be an understatement. Did he really just call out those of us who were working the hardest, rehearsing the longest, and experiencing the most individual success? Yes, that was exactly what he did. What I realized in that moment—once the shock wore off—was that just because you do something well as an individual doesn't mean you automatically help the entire group. Five or six individuals in a group of one hundred had unintentionally fractured the focus of the entire band and distracted from the overall purpose.

The same can happen in the church. The Holy Spirit matters because He is the One who empowers us to fulfill God's mission—together. For many of us who have grown up in Western culture, we think of an "empowered" life as the exceptional life of one person. But we are not called to be Jason Bourne or John Wayne. We are called to be a community.

The Spirit's empowering comes first in forming a community of believers who live out the Christian life and communicate the gospel message to others. In Acts 2:37-47, Peter explained to his repentant listeners that they had to repent and be baptized in the name of Jesus Christ and then they would receive the Holy Spirit. They did, and they were gathered into a believing people who devoted themselves to study, fellowship, bread-breaking, and prayer. It was this community, not an individual or superstar, that God blessed.

As a community of believers who are living a new life by the Spirit, we are to live in a way that shows others God's kingdom. When outsiders look at the church, they should see an example of what a world looks like where God is in charge. Every action, every meeting, every act by believers gathered together should reveal to a watching world that there is something different and good about our God.

Conclusion

Jesus didn't send us an impersonal presence but a Person when He sent the Holy Spirit. Even more, the Spirit He sent is equal to God Himself, which means that the truth of the Spirit dwelling within us means God Himself dwells within us. The Spirit matters because He makes possible our relationship with God, He reminds us that God is close and not distant, and He empowers us as we take the gospel to the nations.

- -

VOICES FROM *Church History*

"O Lord God, I pray not so much for graces as for the Spirit himself, because I feel his absence, and act by my own spirit in everything. Give me not weak desires but the power of his presence, for this is the surest way to have all his graces, and when I have the seal I have the impression also; He can heal, help, quicken, humble suddenly and easily, can work grace and life effectually, and being eternal he can give grace eternally. Save me from great hindrances, from being content with a little measure of the Spirit, from thinking thou wilt not give me more. When I feel my lack of him, light up life and faith, for when I lose thee I am either in the dark and cannot see thee, or Satan and my natural abilities content me with a little light, so that I seek no further for the Spirit of life. Teach me then what to do…Teach me to find and know fullness of the Spirit only in Jesus."[5]

–Puritan prayer

Devotions

GUIDE FOR TRUTH

John 14:16-17: "And I will ask the Father, and He will give you another Counselor to be with you forever. He is the Spirit of truth."

Truth—that which is actual, real, fact, indisputable. God is truth, and what He says can be trusted (Ps. 33:4). God does not have mixed messages. He cannot lie (Titus 1:2). The truth of His word does not change with each culture or generation. This realization comes both as a challenge and a comfort for the believer.

God can be counted on to be who He says He is and to do what He says He will do. "God in his own being or character is the one who fully conforms to the idea of what God should be: namely, a being who is infinitely perfect in power, in wisdom, in goodness, in lordship over time and space."[6]

As we learn what God has said in His Word, we should recognize it as truth and respond in obedience (1 John 5:2-3). Knowing God's truth when we are in relationship with Him brings about transformation in our lives. There is no separating love for God and obedience to Him (Rom. 12:1-2).

Do you find yourself quick to obey when you recognize God's truth? Or does it usually take you a while? God gives us comfort in that we have not been left to figure out truth for ourselves. Jesus promised that the Holy Spirit—the Spirit of truth—would be sent to His disciples (John 14:16-17). God the Spirit was coming to remind the disciples of all the truth that God the Son had taught them (14:26).

Pause and Reflect

1   How often do you use your experiences as a guide for truth without considering what the Bible says? When was the last time you discovered conflict between the two of those (experience and the Bible)?

- -

2   Take time today to personalize Psalm 86:10-12 as a prayer recognizing God's greatness and truth.

Spirit-Filled Community

2 Corinthians 13:13: "The grace of the Lord Jesus Christ, and the love of God, and the fellowship of the Holy Spirit be with all of you."

As you study truths about the Holy Spirit, be sure to pay attention to the emphasis on the Spirit and the body of Christ. Without the Spirit's work in the lives of believers as a body, there can be no church. There can be a group of people meeting together regularly and accomplishing tasks, but it is the Spirit who is the Giver of gifts that build up the church.

Ephesians 2:13 reminds us that before Christ, we were without hope. We were separated from God. But through His death and the shedding of His blood, we have been brought near. But this isn't just good news for us one by one. Paul goes on to write in the same passage that those who were far apart have been brought together with Christ as the cornerstone (vv. 14-22). Jesus has reconciled us to God. The Spirit continues this work in us by continuing to reconcile us to one another by dwelling in us as individual believers and among us as a community.

Ephesians 2:21-22: "The whole building, being put together by Him, grows into a holy sanctuary in the Lord. You also are being built together for God's dwelling in the Spirit."

Pause and Reflect

1   What kind of impact would it have on your class or group if more of the members were sensitive to the unifying desire and power of the Holy Spirit?

2   It is tempting to think of what others can be doing to be more unified in the church? Today, ask God what you can be doing.

EMPOWERING PRESENCE

Romans 8:10: "Now if Christ is in you, the body is dead because of sin, but the Spirit is life because of righteousness."

Without God, we have no way out of sin. But when we become believers, we have new life. We are empowered to do the good works God has planned for us. *Empowering* means to give someone the power and the authority to accomplish something. Our authority comes not from anything we have done but from Christ's payment for our sins through His death and resurrection.

Romans 8:11: "And if the Spirit of Him who raised Jesus from the dead lives in you, then He who raised Christ from the dead will also bring your mortal bodies to life through His Spirit who lives in you."

Our power comes from the Spirit who lives in us and gives us new life. We are no longer bound to sin because we have God in us bringing life and freedom to our lives. We need the Spirit. We cannot live a spiritual life without Him.

The Holy Spirit's presence in our lives is a mark of Christ's ownership of us. We are promised that He is at work in our lives. We are being transformed into the very image of Christ, and we will be raised as Jesus was.

2 Corinthians 3:17-18: Now the Lord is the Spirit, and where the Spirit of the Lord is, there is freedom. We all, with unveiled faces, are looking as in a mirror at the glory of the Lord and are being transformed into the same image from glory to glory; this is from the Lord who is the Spirit."

Pause and Reflect

1   How have you seen God work out changes in your life since you have become a believer?

- -

2   Francis Chan writes, "Where the Spirit is, there is freedom, not bondage or slavery. In our world that is plagued with death, this is a profound truth that points to real hope."[7] What hope does it give you to have God's promise that He is transforming you and giving you new life?

DISCUSSION QUESTIONS

1   Do you come from a church background that speaks often or little of the Holy Spirit?

2   What comes to mind when you think of the Holy Spirit? What do these images or words reveal about your attitude toward Him?

3   In what ways does the Spirit's role as your Counselor impact your relationship with God? How can we cultivate a stronger sense of the recognition of the Spirit's personhood?

4   What are some practical ways to become more aware of the Holy Spirit's Person, presence, and voice in your life?

5   What is the significance of denying that the Holy Spirit is God? What other Christian doctrines do we lose if the Spirit's deity is minimized or denied?

6   Think about the truth that through the Spirit, God Himself dwells in you. In what ways does this truth comfort you? In what ways does it challenge you?

7   Is it possible to obey God without depending on the Holy Spirit? If not, why do we sometimes seek to obey God without considering our need for the Spirit?

8   How intentional are you in spending time with people closest to you? How do these relationships impact your plans, your schedule, and your priorities? How should understanding the closeness of the Spirit alter our priorities and compel us toward mission to those far away from God?

9   What would change in your congregation if more Christians were conscious of the Person and work of the Holy Spirit?

10   What does your local community see when they look upon your group or church? Do they see a glimpse of God's kingdom or is something else getting their attention?

Chapter 11

The Spirit's Work

The Work of the Holy Spirit

VOICES FROM *the Church*

"The Christian's life in all its aspects—intellectual and ethical, devotional and relational, upsurging in worship and outgoing in witness—is supernatural; only the Spirit can initiate and sustain it. So apart from him, not only will there be no lively believers and no lively congregations, there will be no believers and no congregations at all."[1]

–J. I. Packer

VOICES FROM *Church History*

"There is no use in running before you are sent; there is no use in attempting to do God's work without God's power. A man working without this unction, a man working without this anointing, a man working without the Holy Ghost upon him, is losing time after all."[2]

–D. L. Moody (1837-1899)

My mom is an exceptional housekeeper. When I bought my first home and prepared for her first extended visit, I worked myself into a frenzy cleaning the house. Rehearsing in my mind our Saturday morning routines, I cleaned everything I could think of: baseboards, under the sinks, closets. The first morning I went back to work, I was smug at the thought of her spending the day in a clean house!

The smugness disappeared when I got home. I found her resting after a long day of (you guessed it!) cleaning my house. She had worked herself to exhaustion helping me get everything back in order. I distinctly remember her loving lecture on the dangers of neglecting the metal rim around my sink. Then she presented me with a gift—a canister vacuum to have handy for the tile floor.

My mom's close personal inspection revealed dirt I did not see. Her work on my behalf cleaned the house well beyond anything I could do, and then her training and gifts equipped me to carry on the task. Even now, my house is always cleanest when my mom is in town.

Previously we looked at who the Holy Spirit is. Here we will focus on what He does. Just as there is often confusion about the Person of the Spirit, we must be careful to avoid confusion about the work of the Spirit.

In this chapter, we will see that the Holy Spirit has three primary roles in a Christian's life. He reveals our sin to us and points us to Christ. He purifies us and makes us more like Christ. And He empowers us as we embark on mission with the message of Christ. As Christians, we are called to follow the Spirit's leading, cooperate with His activity, and rely on His strength as we point others to Jesus.

The Holy Spirit reveals (John 16:8-11).

8 *When He comes, He will convict the world about sin, righteousness, and judgment:* 9 *about sin, because they do not believe in Me;* 10 *about righteousness, because I am going to the Father and you will no longer see Me;* 11 *and about judgment, because the ruler of this world has been judged.*

The Holy Spirit is the Revealer. According to this passage, the Spirit reveals three things: our sin, God's righteousness, and judgment.

In convicting us about sin, the Spirit is revealing to us how we have chosen to make our own law rather than take God at His Word. The Holy Spirit clarifies what is truth, what is a lie, and what is distorted. How? By bringing the light of God's truth to our lives (John 16:13).

The Holy Spirit shows us the sin we don't see on our own. Sure, we might clean ourselves up and think we're okay by the world's standards, but the Spirit wants to go deeper. As we dig deep into the Scriptures, He digs deep down into our hearts, revealing insights from the Word that not only comfort and inspire us but also expose our sin and drive us to our knees in repentance.

The Holy Spirit shines the light of Scripture on the reality of our situation. That's when the dirt (sin) in our lives becomes much clearer. Once He reveals to us God's righteous perfection, we see with new eyes. We are made aware of how we have fallen short of God's perfect standards.

The Holy Spirit doesn't just reveal our sin; He also reveals the meaning of God's Word to us. Speaking of the Holy Spirit, Jesus said: "The Counselor, the Holy Spirit—the Father will send Him in My name—will teach you all things and remind you of everything I have told you" (14:26). This means that the Spirit does more than shine a light on our hearts. He also shines light on God's Word and opens our minds to help us understand what God has written.

Notice the name that Jesus gave to the Holy Spirit—the Counselor. The emphasis here is on His nearness. The Spirit comes to reveal God's Word and remind us what Jesus taught. He is our Advocate, our Helper, and our Comforter. These titles all imply God's nearness to us through the Spirit bringing to mind the truths of God's Word. That's why anyone who claims some sort of spiritual revelation that is out of line with Scripture is not hearing from God. The Spirit reveals God's Word.

You may be wondering, *How does this work out in my day-to-day life?* Yes, the Holy Spirit reveals our sin, and yes, He reveals God's Word. But how can I be sure that I am following His will? How can we recognize something as God's will rather than our own desires? The good news is that the Holy Spirit guides our steps by reminding us about the character of God and what He has said.

Loving parents don't expect their children to be paralyzed with fear, waiting for permission before every decision. They form their children, teach them the ways of the family, and guide them as they grow up and encounter life's issues. At times, clear direction is given. Other times, parents expect their children to use wisdom in making choices. Children learn to apply what they've seen modeled from their parents.

In a similar manner, when we walk in the Spirit and are open to His illumination of God's Word to us, we walk faithfully—in relationship with the one God. Discovering God's will is not meant to paralyze us with the fear of making a mistake. God intends us to apply what we've learned and to be guided by the Spirit as we make choices in line with His character as revealed in His Word.

The example of Paul in Acts 16:6-7 is instructive here. The missionaries were on the move, seeking to obey God and remain sensitive to the work of the Holy Spirit. They were not on the sidelines waiting for a magical sign. But God intervened and "prevented" them "from speaking the message in Asia. When they came to Mysia, they tried to go into Bithynia, but the Spirit of Jesus did not allow them."

Do you see how the Spirit guided the missionaries? They didn't stay paralyzed in fear, but neither were they so tied to their own plan that they couldn't change course when the Spirit prompted them to do something different.

We aren't meant to walk this path alone. God's will is discerned in community with other believers. We listen to godly counsel. We search the Scriptures. We submit to the Spirit's leading. Certainty and sincerity do not equal "Holy Spirit led." The Spirit-inspired Scriptures are the final authority.

Isn't it great to know the Revealer? The Holy Spirit has revealed the greatness of God and the severity of our sin so He can then show us the reality of God's grace through the power of Christ's death and resurrection.

The Holy Spirit purifies (1 Cor. 6:9-11).

9 *Don't you know that the unrighteous will not inherit God's kingdom? Do not be deceived: No sexually immoral people, idolaters, adulterers, or anyone practicing homosexuality,* 10 *no thieves, greedy people, drunkards, verbally abusive people, or swindlers will inherit God's kingdom.* 11 *And some of you used to be like this. But you were washed, you were sanctified, you were justified in the name of the Lord Jesus Christ and by the Spirit of our God.*

"You were washed." What beautiful words! After listing a number of sinful actions and attitudes, the apostle Paul turned to the beauty of salvation that cleanses us. He made it clear that our washing, our sanctification, and our justification are by the Spirit of our God. When we repent and believe, the Spirit starts the long process of making us holy.

I mentioned earlier about my mother's desire to keep a clean house. But a home can be dirty in more than one way. Have you ever seen one of the television shows about people who hoard their possessions? Often they can't cook, can't have people over, or even sleep in their own beds. There are physical dangers in those homes related to clutter, mold, dirt, and dust. Surprisingly, these individuals are reluctant to let go of items that have no value whatsoever. They mourn the loss of these objects more acutely than the loss of personal relationships and the functionality of their homes.

On the flip side, there are reality shows about housewives who live in homes with elaborate decor, comfortable furnishings, and impeccable physical cleanliness. However, the owners of those homes are also living in their own filth. They invite visitors over just to sabotage them or to gossip about those who don't come. Visits to these homes are more like an emotional chess match. The purpose of these homes is not to glorify God or to serve others but to advance oneself in social circles and in reputation.

What is cluttering your life? Perhaps you are like the hoarder, reluctant to let the Spirit do His purifying work of ridding your heart of worthless, dangerous sins. Or maybe you are like the housewife; everything looks good on the outside but you are beholden to idolatrous desire for power, influence, and privilege.

The Holy Spirit will not leave the Christian alone. He promises to purify us, to clean up our mess, and to get rid of the garbage polluting our lives. Before we came to Christ, we chose our own way. The only way for us to be made clean is through the gospel of Jesus and the power of the Holy Spirit.

As believers, we continue to depend on the Holy Spirit's work to purify us from whatever contaminates us. This purifying, cleansing work of the Holy Spirit is good work. And it is clearly something we cannot do on our own. But we do participate in the process of sanctification.

Because of the Holy Spirit, we can say, "This is who I was, but this is who I am." We cooperate with the Spirit as He purifies us and makes us like Jesus. Paul wrote, "So then, my dear friends, just as you have always obeyed, not only in my presence, but now even more in my absence, work out your own salvation with fear and trembling. For it is God who is working in you, enabling you both to desire and to work out His good purpose" (Phil. 2:12-13). If I could summarize Paul's message here, it would be this: Work, because He's working. Find your identity in Jesus Christ, the One whose reflection is becoming more prominent in your life.

Purification is often a painful experience because it removes from our lives things that once gave us comfort or identity. No longer are we known for our sins, our bad habits, our wrong attitudes or desires. Instead, we are known for who we are in Christ! And all the other things in which we used to find our comfort and identity are being gradually stripped away.

Sanctification (being made holy) is not about us trying to become something we're not. It's about being empowered by the Holy Spirit to embrace who we truly are. If we've been washed, why would we start to bring filthy clutter back into our lives? We are no longer slaves to the sin that once controlled us, but because we live in a fallen world, we will continue to be tempted. That's why we must rely on the Spirit's power as He cleanses us and makes us more like Christ.

As Christians, we are called to respond to the Spirit's revelation and purification. We do not obey to perform or to earn more of His work. We obey in response. Just as the Holy Spirit changes what we see and believe is reality, He also enables us to live in this new reality.

When we live in light of God's purifying work in us, we become sensitive to sin and grow accustomed to living in holiness. When we find filth where we expect cleanliness, we are startled; we are uncomfortable. That is because the Spirit convicts us of sin.

Sanctification is a growing awareness of God's goodness, God's greatness, and God's desires. We become more sensitive to what is not good for us. This is not a passive game. It's aggressive. We are active participants.

Clutter and filth have to be removed from a home before its rooms become useful and welcoming. So let's stop returning to the useless, filthy clutter of sin in our lives—the clutter of fearfulness, prejudice, ambition, competition, excitement, bitterness, etc. Instead, let's yield to the Spirit's work in delivering us from the presence of sin.

The Holy Spirit empowers (Acts 1:4-8).

4 *While He was together with them, He commanded them not to leave Jerusalem, but to wait for the Father's promise. "This," He said, "is what you heard from Me;* 5 *for John baptized with water, but you will be baptized with the Holy Spirit not many days from now."*

6 *So when they had come together, they asked Him, "Lord, are You restoring the kingdom to Israel at this time?"*

7 *He said to them, "It is not for you to know times or periods that the Father has set by His own authority.* 8 *But you will receive power when the Holy Spirit has come on you, and you will be My witnesses in Jerusalem, in all Judea and Samaria, and to the ends of the earth."*

In this passage, we see Jesus reaffirming His promise of the Holy Spirit, whose coming would signal the new reality of God living in the hearts of His people. Throughout the Scriptures, we see God seeking to once again be with His people. He walked through the garden of Eden and called out to Adam when he was hiding because of his sin. He met Moses on the mountain and filled the tabernacle and then the temple in Jerusalem with His presence. At Pentecost, He took up residence in the hearts of His people, and at the end of time, He will be with us forever: "Look! God's dwelling is with humanity, and He will live with them. They will be His people, and God Himself will be with them and be their God" (Rev. 21:3).

Sometimes people look at the promise of the Holy Spirit indwelling believers and wonder if the Holy Spirit had any real involvement in the Old Testament. He did. In the Old Testament, the Holy Spirit empowered certain individuals for special service. King David is one example: "So Samuel took the horn of oil, anointed him in the presence of his brothers, and the Spirit of the LORD took control of David from that day forward" (1 Sam. 16:13).

In the New Testament, the Spirit gives life (John 6:63). Jesus said, "The Spirit is the One who gives life. The flesh doesn't help at all. The words that I have spoken to you are spirit and are life." The Spirit gives us power to be Christ's ambassadors. Yielding to the Spirit's control, we are given a spiritual power that we cannot generate or imitate on our own. We are dependent upon Him.

The Holy Spirit is the One who gives us new life and power for our work. For our work to have eternal and spiritual impact, it has to be empowered by the Holy Spirit. We might imitate the work of the Spirit, but a replica does not carry the same value nor the same power as the original. Imitation of the Holy Spirit's work may share a resemblance, but it will lack the power of God.

The passage in Acts 1 reminds us that the truth about the Spirit revealing our sin and purifying us isn't meant to stop with our own sanctification. The promised Holy Spirit comes, indwells believers, and brings power so that we might be a community that actively witnesses to our faith in Jesus Christ. Yes, we need His power in order to walk with God as we ought. But we also need His power in order to fulfill the mission God has given us.

The Holy Spirit is not merely given for our personal benefit but for our missional empowerment. The Spirit fills us in order that we might fill the world with gospel proclamation. We are empowered not to do whatever we want and hand it over to God but to serve others and fulfill the mission He has laid out for us.

The Holy Spirit was sent for a purpose and not for our amusement or satisfaction. He is our Comforter, our Guide, and our Counselor. Yet His presence is not there just to benefit us but to fulfill God's purpose. His power reveals our sin, purifies our hearts, and enables our engagement in His mission. He is the Comforter who calls us to give up comfort for His mission.

Too many times we think of empowerment as being about us, as if it were about what advances us and gives us an advantage. But the Holy Spirit's empowerment is about advancing the kingdom of God and the name of Jesus Christ. It's not about us or our willpower but about God getting glory.

Conclusion

One way we can see the importance of the Spirit's work is to imagine our Christian walk without Him. Where would we be without the Holy Spirit? Who would bring to our attention our remaining sin? How would we understand the Bible? Who would make us look more like Christ?

Where would we get the boldness, passion, and power to proclaim the gospel? Without the Spirit, we are still blind, still in our sin, and powerless to fulfill God's mission. But with the Spirit, we can move forward with hope.

Michael Kelley reminds us of the joy in putting our faith in God as He makes us more like Jesus: "Once again, we find faith as the central work of the Christian. What about you? Do you believe what the Bible says about you? That you're a saint? A son? A daughter? The righteousness of Christ? Work hard at believing these things to be true. Work hard at believing you've been transformed. While you're working hard to believe, the Holy Spirit is working hard, too. He's busy sanctifying you, prying the remnants of who you used to be out of the grasp of the child of God you are now. He's working hard to transform you into who you've already become in Christ." [3]

Devotions

THE UNCOMFORTABLE COMFORTER

Romans 14:17: "For the kingdom of God is not eating and drinking, but righteousness, peace, and joy in the Holy Spirit."

I'm a big fan of "comfortable," and I work hard to make sure things around me are just right: shoes, desk chairs, thermostats, even God. Oftentimes I find that what I expect from God is comfort—no ups or downs, just steady. I sit expectantly like Goldilocks, looking for how God can make my life "just right."

However, the reality is that when God is at work in our lives, we often don't find ourselves in a stock photo moment—with everything turning out "just right." The Holy Spirit, as Comforter, can come in and make us uncomfortable:

- We seek comfort in success; He brings us an opportunity to serve.
- We long for love and adoration from others; He opens the door for us to submit.
- We pray for the Spirit's blessing on our ministry and efforts; He changes the plan, or He blesses and bears fruit, but someone else gets the credit.

When we are focused on ourselves and not God's mission, we look for the wrong results. God is ready to do amazing works in our lives, but we risk missing out if our expectations are not in line with His will.

Pause and Reflect

1 Have you sensed God's closeness and work in your life even when it was uncomfortable?

2 Read Romans 5:3-5. In what situations can we know we will find comfort from God?

3 How have you been comforted by God during a difficult time in your life?

REMEMBER EVERYTHING!

John 14:26: "But the Counselor, the Holy Spirit—the Father will send Him in My name—will teach you all things and remind you of everything I have told you."

Do you have a good friend or family member that you can count on to always tell the truth? You know they will tell you difficult news even though it isn't what you want to hear. Good counselors don't just bring the tough news, they also bring good news. When we are focused too narrowly on a negative situation, they broaden the horizon and put things in perspective. They help us see the good that can be hiding out in our blind spots.

In this chapter we see that the Holy Spirit reveals, purifies, and empowers us. It is tempting to get discouraged by the hard part of that teaching. We also need to remember that the Spirit is at work reminding us of God's truth, God's goodness, God's completed work of redemption in Christ, and God's provision to empower our new life.

It can be easy to let conviction lead to discouragement if we forget that the Holy Spirit is reminding us of the gospel. We are no longer separated from God (John 14:6); Jesus is our Lord (Rom. 10:9-10); salvation is a freely given gift (Eph. 2:8-9); we are free from the shame of our past sin (Rom. 10:11-12).

The Holy Spirit's work reminds us that we are living our lives in the truth of who we are in Christ. This is a new life, a fresh start, a spiritual life that is empowered by God. Don't let the conviction of sin and the purifying work of the Holy Spirit blind you to the good news of your new life in Christ. Celebrate the good news.

Pause and Reflect

1   What good things about God are you quick to forget?

----

2   Whom could you call or email right now with a word of encouragement that reminds them of God's goodness and faithfulness?

MOVING OUT ON MISSION

Acts 16:7: "When they came to Mysia, they tried to go into Bithynia, but the Spirit of Jesus did not allow them."

Sometimes I get tired of hearing from people who only critique others' work when they themselves are not engaged at all. Critiquing someone from experience is one thing; critiquing someone from knowledge alone is quite another. In other words, they're saying, "I've read a lot of books on the topic, and if I did that, I would do it differently." But often they aren't doing anything—except reading more books, blogs, and twitter feeds.

Life, experience, and reality can pass us by when we are so focused on the spiritual that we never put on work clothes. The apostle Paul was well-trained, well-educated, and well-known. But he was also incredibly busy doing what he was called to do. He was going. He was starting churches. He was preaching the gospel. In the midst of going, he was seeking guidance from the Holy Spirit. And in the midst of going, the Spirit would sometimes redirect Paul.

Are you waiting for God's big plans to come to you? Or are you acting on what you already know? Are you sensitive to the Spirit as you serve and obey?

Pause and Reflect

1   Paul describes the life of a believer in very active terms: fighter, runner, soldier (2 Tim. 4:7; Phil 2:25). What three words would you use to describe your life as a believer? Do they tend to be more active or passive?

2   Can you identify any selfish pursuits that take your focus off of others? Ask God to show you how to shift your focus toward others. What could you specifically do today?

DISCUSSION QUESTIONS

1   As you progress spiritually, are you more inclined to notice additional sins that need to be rooted out? Why or why not? How can you become aware of the sinful residue and dirt that remains in your life? How should we respond when we discover hidden sin?

2   Are you thankful when the Spirit convicts you of sin? What is the difference between the Holy Spirit's conviction of sin and having a guilty conscience?

3   In what ways is our evangelism affected by the truth that the Holy Spirit is the One who convicts of sin?

4   What are some wrong impressions we may have about how the Holy Spirit guides us? What should we do when two believers have conflicting views of what God's will is in a particular situation?

5   How does our work and God's work in sanctification fit together? How does knowing your true identity in Christ change the way you view sanctification?

6   Discuss the popular phrase "Let go and let God." How might this slogan downplay our need to be active in pursuing holiness?

7   Do our lives and churches look like they are led by the Holy Spirit? How can we ensure that people looking at our church see a people who reflect God's kingdom? What are some practical ways to stand apart from the world?

8   Why might Christians be tempted to obey God in their own strength rather than in the power of the Spirit? How can we increase our dependence on the Spirit's power? What are some comforts that you might need to put aside as you rely more heavily upon the Comforter?

9   If you knew complete dependence on the Holy Spirit would mean less of a reputation but more eternal impact, would you desire it? How can a church make sure that its activities are motivated by a desire to see God's kingdom advanced?

Chapter 12

God in Us

The Fruit and Gifts of the Spirit

VOICES FROM *the Church*

"The more I know [Christ], the more I love Him. The more I love Him, the more I obey Him. The more I obey Him, the more I become like Him. The more I become like Him, the better I know Him. The better I know Him, I love Him the more. And the more I love Him, I reach a new level of likeness to Him." [1]
–Robertson McQuilkin

VOICES FROM *Church History*

"It is absurd to imagine that God should justify a people, and they should still go on in sin. If God should justify a people and not sanctify them, he would justify a people whom he could not glorify." [2]
–Thomas Watson (1620-1686)

Much to my father's delight, I was a gullible child, which gave him the opportunity to have some fun with me. During one family vacation, he convinced me that he could stop the rain by clapping his hands. He would make sure I was paying attention, then briefly take his hands off the steering wheel to clap. Sure enough, every time, the rain stopped for a moment. (Later he explained that we were driving under an overpass when he would clap!)

Kids don't understand many things. They learn some things just by watching and observing the world. But there are other things (like world history, science, math, etc.) that need to be described for them. They would never know the significance of Abraham Lincoln's life if it weren't for history books and people to interpret them. Kids need someone to tell them things if they are to grow in knowledge and understanding.

In a similar way, we need the Holy Spirit to reveal God's truth to us. We can't grow spiritually without His work in our lives. We're like kids who can see the world but fail to make the proper connections. We lack understanding, especially when it comes to spiritual truth, until the Holy Spirit guides us and teaches us. As believers, we need God to work in us to shape us into the people He has called us to be.

The Holy Spirit's work in us is past, present, and future. His work begins by convicting us of our sin and changing our hearts. His work continues as He bears fruit in our lives and gives us gifts for the good of God's people on mission in the world. Best of all, we look ahead to the day when the Spirit's work will be complete. In the meantime, we celebrate the Spirit's fruit and exercise His gifts as we seek to live faithfully in light of the gospel.

The Spirit begins God's work in us (John 3:1-8).

1 *There was a man from the Pharisees named Nicodemus, a ruler of the Jews.* 2 *This man came to Him at night and said, "Rabbi, we know that You have come from God as a teacher, for no one could perform these signs You do unless God were with him."*

3 *Jesus replied, "I assure you: Unless someone is born again, he cannot see the kingdom of God."*

4 *"But how can anyone be born when he is old?" Nicodemus asked Him. "Can he enter his mother's womb a second time and be born?"*

5 *Jesus answered, "I assure you: Unless someone is born of water and the Spirit, he cannot enter the kingdom of God.* 6 *Whatever is born of the flesh is flesh, and whatever is born of the Spirit is spirit.* 7 *Do not be amazed that I told you that you must be born again.* 8 *The wind blows where it pleases, and you hear its sound, but you don't know where it comes from or where it is going. So it is with everyone born of the Spirit."*

Have you ever stopped to think about how strange the gospel message is? "Gospel" means "good news," but this news about Jesus certainly isn't intuitive. No one naturally gravitates to a faith with a bloody cross at the center. In a scientific age, how is it that millions of people continue to find compelling the story of a dead man walking out of His grave? This isn't the kind of message we'd dream up, is it? So how do we explain the fact that people all over the world have had their hearts gripped by this gospel?

The only answer is the Holy Spirit. He is the One who powerfully reveals the power of the gospel. It is the Holy Spirit who begins God's work in us.

Many people (even in the church!) are like Nicodemus. We may have knowledge of God. We may claim some sort of religious identity. We may be curious about certain aspects of our faith. But some of us haven't figured out what the big deal is about Jesus.

Do you see how Nicodemus was puzzled by the claims of Christ? Yes, he knew enough about God to see Him at work in the ministry of Jesus. He recognized Jesus' work because it reflected God's character and nature. He also affirmed that the things he had seen and heard from Jesus could only be from God. But he wasn't fully committed yet. Nicodemus knew truth about Jesus, but merely knowing truth wasn't enough to change his life.

When we look at Jesus' interactions throughout the Gospels, we find that He did not employ a one-size-fits-all method of conversation. He often explained the same truths about salvation differently to different people.

For Nicodemus, Jesus chose to emphasize that salvation is spiritual and supernatural. It is impossible to receive salvation merely through religious works. Jesus was explaining that Nicodemus could not be saved by his own effort. He needed to be born from above. In other words, salvation is not something we make happen; it is something that happens to us. We respond with repentance and faith to the Holy Spirit's calling.

The work of God in us begins with the Holy Spirit convicting us of our sin and showing us our need for a Savior. Salvation is about being "born again," "born from above." It's a birth brought about by the Holy Spirit.

Jesus pointed out the mysterious nature of this new birth by using the illustration of the wind. We cannot see the wind, but we do observe the impact it makes. In the same way, we do not understand all the workings of the Holy Spirit at the moment of salvation. (Christians often disagree on the logical order of how it all takes place.) But we certainly see the effect of salvation when a person is brought from death to life, from darkness to light.

The Holy Spirit works through the message of the gospel, blowing the winds of conviction into our hearts. We are called to respond to Him with repentance (turning from sin) and faith (trusting in the work of Christ alone for our salvation). Being "born again," or "regenerated," is not something we can earn with our own good works. We need salvation from above, a spiritual birth that comes from the Holy Spirit Himself.

The Spirit continues God's work in us (Gal. 5:16-26; 1 Cor. 12:4-11).

We've seen how the Holy Spirit begins His work in us. In the next two passages, we will see how the Holy Spirit continues His work by bearing fruit in our lives and by giving us gifts for His mission. Let's start with the fruit of the Spirit in Galatians 5:

16 *I say then, walk by the Spirit and you will not carry out the desire of the flesh.* 17 *For the flesh desires what is against the Spirit, and the Spirit desires what is against the flesh; these are opposed to each other, so that you don't do what you want.* 18 *But if you are led by the Spirit, you are not under the law.*

19 *Now the works of the flesh are obvious: sexual immorality, moral impurity, promiscuity,* 20 *idolatry, sorcery, hatreds, strife, jealousy, outbursts of anger, selfish ambitions, dissensions, factions,* 21 *envy, drunkenness, carousing, and anything similar. I tell you about these things in advance—as I told you before—that those who practice such things will not inherit the kingdom of God.*

22 *But the fruit of the Spirit is love, joy, peace, patience, kindness, goodness, faith,* 23 *gentleness, self-control. Against such things there is no law.* 24 *Now those who belong to Christ Jesus have crucified the flesh with its passions and desires.* 25 *Since we live by the Spirit, we must also follow the Spirit.* 26 *We must not become conceited, provoking one another, envying one another.*

Fruit of the Spirit

If you're like me, you may look over some of these works of the flesh and think, *Whew! Glad I don't have trouble with those!* But maybe we should take a closer look. There are sins listed here that are familiar to all of us.

The works of the flesh focus on self. They're all about doing things our way. These are the kinds of sins that separate us from God and hinder us from having healthy relationships with others. The works of the flesh come naturally to those who do not know Christ.

But as Christians, we are to be led by the Spirit. The Spirit changes everything. Paul even switches terminology, using "works" (plural) in reference to the flesh and "fruit" (singular) in reference to the Spirit.

Good fruit is satisfying, a delight to the taste buds. If you've ever spent any time gardening, you know how wonderful it is to taste the fruit of your labor. You also know that even though you may tend the garden and nurture it, you cannot produce fruit on your own. In the same way, spiritual fruit is not something we work up by our own power. Spiritual fruit is something the Spirit works out in us by His power. Fruit is produced by the Holy Spirit. We can nurture the circumstances for growth, but it is the Holy Spirit who is working out Christ's character in us. The fruit of the Spirit is what the Spirit does in us.

Bearing fruit is not the same thing as buying fruit and handing it out to others. Take "gentleness" as an example. Many Christians think of the Christian life in terms of gritted teeth and forced obedience. But there is a difference between gentleness that comes naturally (or should we say supernaturally) by the work of the Spirit and gentleness that is forced and obligated. The actions may look similar, but one person is free to be gentle, while the other is forced. One is external, while the other flows from the heart.

Now let's turn to the gifts that the Holy Spirit gives us, gifts that are intended to equip us for God's mission. In 1 Corinthians 12:4-11, Paul writes:

4 *Now there are different gifts, but the same Spirit.* 5 *There are different ministries, but the same Lord.* 6 *And there are different activities, but the same God activates each gift in each person.* 7 *A demonstration of the Spirit is given to each person to produce what is beneficial:*
8 *to one is given a message of wisdom*
through the Spirit,
to another, a message of knowledge
by the same Spirit,
9 *to another, faith by the same Spirit,*
to another, gifts of healing by the one Spirit,
10 *to another, the performing of miracles,*
to another, prophecy,
to another, distinguishing between spirits,
to another, different kinds of languages,
to another, interpretation of languages.
11 *But one and the same Spirit is active in all these, distributing to each person as He wills.*

Gifts of the Spirit

Spiritual gifts can be defined as "any ability that is empowered by the Holy Spirit and used in any ministry of the church."[3] These abilities can be of the more miraculous sort (as listed in 1 Cor. 12:8-10), but they can also be Spirit-empowered natural abilities, as seen in other lists: Romans 12:6-8; 1 Corinthians 12:28; Ephesians 4:11; and 1 Peter 4:10-11.

First Corinthians 12:7 makes it clear that each believer is given a gift of the Spirit (perhaps more than one) for the purpose of producing what is beneficial. Beneficial for whom? For the body of believers and, by extension, the world in need of Jesus (12:12-31). The Holy Spirit gives gifts to edify, or build up, the church and to equip her for mission. Believers ought to discover their gift(s) so they can participate in the body and mission of Christ. Not to do so means denying yourself the joy of service and depriving the church and others of the grace, love, and Spirit-empowered abilities given by the Spirit for their benefit.

Over and over again, we see Paul make reference to God the Spirit: the "same Spirit" (v. 4); the "same Lord" (v. 5); the "same God" (v. 6). And then the Spirit is explicitly mentioned in verse 7, twice in verse 8, twice in verse 9, and again in verse 11. Sounds like Paul was trying to tell us something, doesn't it?

The Holy Spirit gives gifts to edify the church and equip her for mission. Too many times we jump right into controversies about spiritual gifts or we immediately begin filling out spiritual gift surveys to see where we might fit in. Instead, we should remember that focusing on our spiritual gifts without grounding those gifts in the knowledge of the Giver—God the Spirit—will lead us to miss out on the joy of knowing God.

Furthermore, the major point of this passage is that the diversity of gifts is for the good of the church. It's not just so that we know God but that others in the church come to see God at work in us. The ultimate goal is that people outside the church will come to know God as well.

The Spirit is intentional in how He gives these gifts to His people. The intention is mission-focused in that the gifts are meant to build up the church in order that God's mission be carried forward.

When we engage in ministry that allows us to use our spiritual gifts, we must be careful to keep the mission at the forefront—the glory of God, not the glory of our own name. Whenever we use our gifts in a way that elevates us instead of edifying the church or when the gifts make us look good instead of making God look glorious, we have a problem.

Notice also that the Spirit is the One who directs the use of these gifts. As we live with others in community, seeking to obey Christ, we want to utilize our gifts and find a place of service. What we must never do is demand and direct the use of our gifts. Gifts are not given for our own personal benefit and fulfillment; they are given to us for the church.

Sometimes Christians will try to "fake" the fruit of the Spirit or "fake" the exercise of spiritual gifts. In other words, we will put on a mask and try to show others how well we can hold everything together. But seeking to look good in front of others is a work of the flesh, not the Spirit. Those closest to us will inevitably see our hypocrisy. Have you ever smelled fake fruit? It is manufactured, not organic. (And it gives off a stench!)

Trying to live the Christian life in our own power is an exhausting, spiritually debilitating process. Think about a field that is overused. When the ground is never allowed to rest and the farmer never rotates crops, the soil loses critical nutrients and the usefulness of the field is damaged. In a similar way, Christians who seek to exercise spiritual gifts or bear spiritual fruit in their own power will become focused on their performance. Their good deeds will not be out of an abundance from walking by the Holy Spirit but out of performance from walking in the flesh.

So what should we do in order to bear fruit rather than perform works? Michael Kelley answers this with the illustration of different kinds of boats.

- *Rowboat* Christians believe their spiritual lives are all about effort. They're the ones holding the oars. They're the ones extending themselves and exhausting themselves.
- *Bass boat* Christians just turn the key and let the motor work, thinking the Christian doesn't need to do anything at all. "Just let go and let God" as the saying goes.
- *Sailboat* Christians, however, are about yielding control. Michael writes: "The forward motion of a sailboat is based exclusively on catching the wind. No wind, no motion. You can't control the wind. You can, however, control the sail. Your job as the sailor is to tie the sail correctly. You point the boat in the right direction and raise the sail up the mast."[4]

When we exercise our spiritual gifts and involve ourselves in spiritual disciplines, we are raising the sail and reading the boat, and we yield control to the Spirit who works in us.

The Spirit will complete God's work in us (Eph. 1:13-14).

13 *When you heard the message of truth, the gospel of your salvation, and when you believed in Him, you were also sealed with the promised Holy Spirit.* 14 *He is the down payment of our inheritance, for the redemption of the possession, to the praise of His glory.*

In this passage, Paul used the illustration of a "seal." We are sealed with the Holy Spirit. His presence in our lives today is the guarantee for our lives tomorrow. The seal gives us confidence in the present and provides hope for the future. He continues to work in us and to keep us, comfort us, and guide us. And the day is coming when the Spirit will complete His work in us.

In 2 Corinthians 1:21-22, Paul once again used the illustration of being sealed: "Now it is God who strengthens us, with you, in Christ and has anointed us. He has also sealed us and given us the Spirit as a down payment in our hearts." In the Father, we are strengthened; in the Son, we are anointed; and in the Spirit, we are sealed with a down payment and guarantee of our hope and heavenly inheritance.

The seal reminds us that God is King and that He assures us of the future hope. We as believers have not yet experienced the fullness of the kingdom of God, but through the work of the Spirit, we have a foretaste of what is promised for the future. There is a plan. There is a purpose. Best of all, there is a Person at work. And through Him—the Holy Spirit—we look boldly toward our future hope.

Conclusion

In this session, we've looked at the Holy Spirit's work in us—past, present, and future. His work in us is not merely for our personal benefit but also for our engagement in God's mission:

• Since the Spirit is the One who convicts people of sin, we ought to fervently pray for the lost, knowing that God is the One who has the power to save.
• Since the Spirit is the One who continues His work in us, we ought to bear the fruit of the Spirit as a testimony to His power and exercise spiritual gifts in a way that equips the church to better fulfill her mission.
• Since the Spirit is the One who will complete His work in us, we can move forward with confidence that the purposes of the Lord will be fulfilled. The future is assured, and we can move toward that future with faith, hope, and love.

Devotions

SOIL TEST

Read the Parable of the Sower in Matthew 13:1-9: "As he was sowing, some seed...fell among thorns, and the thorns came up and choked them."

Simple, regular yard work is one of the most renewing and fulfilling tasks of homeownership, or so I've heard. I actually don't care for it at all. Recently, out of a little bit of shame and newfound frugality, I decided to take on the weed crisis that has overcome my yard. I tackled the weeds just a little every day so as not to startle the neighbors with a drastic change. At first, I was frustrated at how quickly it seemed the weeds could grow back. But more recently, I've been encouraged that with the rain, grass is now thriving where once there were only weeds. The weeds had been taking up all the soil and soaking up all the rain. Now that they are gone, the grass is unstoppable.

When we look for the Spirit's work in our lives (fruit and gifts), it's important that we remember: fruit is free to flourish when we are faithful in letting the Spirit "weed" out the things in our lives that choke the fruit. We must remove the things in our lives that make us comfortable yet unfruitful. Just as weeding a yard feels like a chore and can easily be put off, so we as believers tend to avoid dealing with the things in our lives that are choking out His desire to bear fruit through us.

Pause and Reflect

1   In what ways are you stubborn and resistant to God's work in your life?

- -

2   Think of a time when you enthusiastically decided to obey God but faltered once you experienced a challenge.

- -

3   What is something in your life that on the surface feels comfortable and necessary but is hindering what God wants to do through you?

Look Out for Number One

Philippians 2:4: "Everyone should look out not only for his own interests, but also for the interests of others."

We know that as Christians we are to serve and help others, but who gets to decide? Are we supposed to help everyone that asks? What is the "best" cause or ministry? Where do we start?

The apostle Paul gives us clarity in his Letter to the church at Philippi. In chapter 2, Paul reminded them of their goal and what they needed to do to achieve it. Their goal was unity. That unity would bring encouragement in Christ, fellowship with the Spirit, and love. Achieving that goal would also fulfill Paul's joy. How were they to accomplish this? They had to humble themselves, focus on meeting one another's needs, and take on the attitude of Christ.

Paul went on in that chapter to remind them of their work—yes, work! Unity requires work without grumbling and arguing. The only way we can do this is by looking first to God—not others. Our service and focus on others has to spring from God's heart first. When we are satisfied in Christ, empowered by the Spirit, and in awe of the Father, we have the best posture and attitude for serving others. Whenever we fail to focus on God, we set ourselves down a path of "service" that will be cluttered with competition and rivalry.

Pause and Reflect

1   Think of a time when you served others and found it to be a difficult experience. In your opinion, what robbed you of joy in that experience?

---

2   Can you think of fears you have when you are asked to serve others? Fear of being taken advantage of? Fear of being slowed down on your other goals? Fear of missing out on a better opportunity?

---

3   Think of a time you had a great experience serving others. What was it that made that experience so good?

THE GIFT RECEIPT

There is one type of reality TV show that I can't sit through—the spoiled teenager birthday one. The few I have seen always show a number of adults in a frenzy to create a magical, memorable event for a painfully ungrateful teen. Inevitably, there is a big angry rant by the teenager and teary parents wondering how they could have purchased the wrong luxury car. When I watch these, I do not have nurturing thoughts toward those teenagers. But neither do I have them toward myself.

Ingratitude is not only a symptom of the financially privileged. It runs rampant in the spiritually privileged as well. In 1 Corinthians 12:4-11, Paul tells us there are indeed different gifts and ministries, such as wisdom, knowledge, healing, and discernment. How often do we become like a spoiled reality TV teenager fixated on our "lack" of the gifts God has given to others and completely dissatisfied with (or unaware of) the gifts we've been given?

It would take out the sting (and probably the ratings) to see one of these reality TV teenagers focus on family and friends during these events rather than on a self-centered quest of accumulation. But again, how different are we than these teens? Paul tells us that, yes, there are many gifts, but they are given by One God: "To [one], faith by the same Spirit, to another, gifts of healing by the one Spirit...But one and the same Spirit is active in all these, distributing to each person as He wills" (vv. 9,11).

It is the Spirit's choice to give gifts to His people, so let's move away from making gifts our focus. Let's look to the Giver of gifts for our satisfaction. Let's use the gifts we've been given to build up the body of Christ.

Pause and Reflect

1   Read 1 Corinthians 12:12-31. Ask God to show you any ways that you have failed to use His gifts to benefit others, hoping instead for the gifts that were given to another.

Discussion Questions

1   Think about the mystery of physical growth. What makes us grow? Now consider the mystery of spiritual growth. What must take place for a person to grow spiritually?

2   What is missing in the life of Nicodemus (John 3)? Are his questions a sign of openness to Jesus? How does Jesus' kind but firm response to Nicodemus provide a model for how we engage with those who are spiritually minded but not committed to Christ?

3   Can you think of a time when you were as frustrated as Nicodemus seems to be in this passage, seeking to know God but unable to fully understand Him? How can we be encouraged when we are faced with things that first seem mysterious?

4   Why is it important to remember that conviction over our sin is something the Spirit works in our hearts? How does the truth that conversion is supernatural lead us to pray more fervently for people who do not know Christ?

5   Can you think of any areas where you have been selfish that would fall into one of the "works of the flesh" Paul mentioned in Galatians 5? In what ways have you been seeking satisfaction in these pursuits?

6   How does calling the Spirit's work "fruit" rather than "works" change how we think about our relationship with the Holy Spirit? Where do you see the Holy Spirit bringing out these characteristics in your life?

7   How have you experienced the Holy Spirit bearing fruit in your life? When has God been your source of joy, gentleness, self-control? If you were to examine your church, what fruit of the Spirit would you immediately see? What about works of the flesh?

8   Have you ever taken a spiritual gifts inventory? If so, did it help you serve more effectively in the local church? Have you ever avoided serving when you saw a need because you thought your gift didn't apply? How does the mission of God impact the way we view the Spirit's gifts?

9   In what ways does assurance of the completion of the Spirit's work in our lives give us confidence to live faithfully today?

Chapter 13

The Trinity

The Mystery of One God in Three Persons

Trinity. The word means "tri-unity" or "three-in-oneness." It's the word we use to describe the God of the Bible as being one God in three Persons. The word is easy to say. The concept is difficult to comprehend.

Sometimes in our desire to simplify the concept, we trot out handy illustrations about the Trinity we've heard over the years. But here is where I want to wave a yellow caution flag before we continue. (For the non-NASCAR fan, a yellow flag means a driver should slow down due to hazards on the racetrack!)

When studying complex or weighty subjects in the Bible, we should avoid the temptation to over-simplify the truth. For example, someone could tell the story of the crucifixion and resurrection of Jesus Christ with sock puppets. But unless you're a master puppeteer and gospel communicator who can retain the somber and weighty message of the cross, your additional embellishments would distract from and diminish the powerful message.

Well-intentioned Christians sometimes over-simplify the Trinity by using everyday objects that have three parts (e.g. eggs, apples, and trees). While each does have three distinct parts: the egg (yolk, white, and shell), the apple (seeds, flesh, and skin), and the tree (roots, trunk, branches), these distinct parts are not made of the same substance. No one part can also be called the whole. Likewise, the common illustration that one man can fill three roles (son, husband, and father) undermines the teaching on the Trinity (this example lends itself to the heresy called "modalism").

We always do well to stick with what the Bible says. God is big, God is mysterious, and God is One. The best way to help people understand this truth is to stay with the Scriptures. The goal is that careful study of the Scriptures will eliminate confusion and transform our ponderings into worshipful awe before our triune God.

VOICES FROM *Church History*

"The unity of the Trinity, of the Father and the Son and the Holy Spirit... in no other subject is error more dangerous, or inquiry more laborious, or the discovery of truth more profitable."[3]
–Augustine (354-430)

In this chapter we are going to spend some time on three clear teachings we see in the Bible about God. The word *Trinity* may not be found in the Bible, but the truth is all over its pages. As theologian B. B. Warfield explained, "The doctrine of the Trinity is given to us in Scripture, not in formulated definition, but in fragmentary allusions; when we assemble [them] into their organic unity, we are not passing from Scripture, but entertaining more thoroughly into the meaning of Scripture."[4]

The Bible clearly teaches three things about God: God is One, God is three distinct Persons, and each Person is fully God. When we put this puzzle called the Trinity together, we don't find an abstract theory to be analyzed but a loving God to be adored. The self-giving love of God, reflected in His own unity and diversity, is the basis for our salvation and the motivation for our love for God and neighbor.

There is one God (Deut. 6:4-5).

4 *"Listen, Israel: The LORD our God, the LORD is One.* 5 *Love the LORD your God with all your heart, with all your soul, and with all your strength.*

"The LORD is One." This means that God has no rival, no substitute, no peers. The only appropriate response to God's revelation of Himself is total devotion. It is not enough to know there is only one God. (The demons know that, and shudder!) Instead, this is a foundational truth we must live by. In this Old Testament passage, the truth of God's oneness reminded the Israelites that they could have no competing loyalties—whether idols or other people—when it came to loving God.

In the New Testament, when Jesus was asked by a scribe to select the most important commandment, He quoted this passage: "Listen, Israel! The Lord our God, the Lord is One. Love the Lord your God with all your heart, with all your soul, with all your mind, and with all your strength." Then He added, "The second is: Love your neighbor as yourself. There is no other command greater than these" (Mark 12:28-34).

The Bible is clear that God is One. He is unique and without rival. He deserves our total devotion. If we lose sight of this truth, we will find ourselves distracted, preoccupied, and divided by the other important things jockeying for position in our lives. Rightly recognizing who God is shapes our posture and attitude toward Him. And God's oneness then shapes how we respond to others.

The Lord's uniqueness is one of the Old Testament's main teachings. Consider Isaiah 45:5-6: "I am Yahweh, and there is no other; there is no God but Me. I will strengthen you, though you do not know Me, so that all may know from the rising of the sun to its setting that there is no one but Me. I am Yahweh, and there is no other." As we read the Bible, we see the one true God at work. The great acts of redemption, the creation of the world, and the sustaining of its daily activities—it is God who does it all. Later verses in this same passage from Isaiah remind us that it is not our place to question God. We are created, and He is the Creator (vv. 9-12).

God's uniqueness is tied to His authority. God sought out Israel for relationship. God chose them to be His people, to fulfill His purpose of redemption. This choice was not based on Israel's faithfulness but on God's loving purposes for the world. God is the Lord. He establishes the terms of His relationship with humanity, and He alone can fulfill His promises.

Even though we see throughout the Old Testament the undeniable truth that God is One, there are other affirmations that hint toward *complexity*. While the New Testament provides a greater amount of clarity on the three Persons of the Trinity, the Old Testament is not silent on the subject. The complexity and plurality of the Persons of the Godhead is seen in the earliest chapters of the Bible.

Take a look at how God speaks in Genesis 1:26: "Then God said, 'Let Us make man in Our image, according to Our likeness.'" There are multiple places where God refers to Himself using the plural pronouns "Us" and "Our": "Let Us make man in Our image" (1:26); "Since man has become like one of Us" (3:22); "Come, let Us go down there and confuse their language" (11:7). Later in Isaiah 6:8, we read, "Then I heard the voice of the Lord saying: Who should I send? Who will go for Us?"

Where do these hints lead us? To the next truth we see about God. He is One in three Persons.

Though God is One, He is three Persons (Mark 1:9-11).

While the nature of God still remains complex and to some degree mysterious, the New Testament brings more clarity to our understanding of the Trinity. As we see more places where all three Persons are mentioned, we learn more about their distinct roles. Take a look at Mark 1:9-11.

9 In those days Jesus came from Nazareth in Galilee and was baptized in the Jordan by John. 10 As soon as He came up out of the water, He saw the heavens being torn open and the Spirit descending to Him like a dove. 11 And a voice came from heaven:
You are My beloved Son;
I take delight in You!

In the baptism of Jesus, we see all three Persons of the Trinity in action. Jesus is baptized. The Father speaks from heaven. And the Spirit descends to empower Jesus for His earthly ministry (see Mark 3:22-30). Note the Spirit's descent from the Father (1:10), the love expressed by the Father for the Son (1:11), and the Son's reliance on the Spirit (1:12). Here we see a glimpse of the glorious love at the heart of God. The Father, Son, and Spirit are talking, listening, loving, and delighting in one another.

God is One, and He is three Persons. There is unity of purpose in the three Persons, yet that unity is rooted in love. There is no conflict or jealousy among them. Theologian Bruce Ware writes: "They are always sharing fully the delight in being the one God and accomplishing the unified purpose of God…Each divine Person accepts his role, each in proper relation to the others, and each works together with the others for one unified, common purpose." [5]

God's revelation of Himself in unity and diversity is reflected in human relationships. We are to find our greatest satisfaction in loving God and loving others. Unfortunately, our sin nature causes us to act like the world revolves around us. We use other people who can help us get ahead. We put personal goals before people.

So even though we were created to relate to God and one another perfectly, our relationships have been disrupted. Sin leads us to focus on self. We're at odds with each other. The kind of delight we see between the Members of the Trinity is usually not the kind of love we give and receive.

Fortunately, we don't have to live according to our self-centered flesh. The gospel tells the story of how God the Father loved us enough to send the Son to give us new life. And now, when we repent and believe, we are empowered by the Spirit to be a community of believers who are God-centered, not self-centered. Once we see God at the center of the universe and not ourselves, the joyful love of God between the Father, Son, and Spirit spills over into our human relationships as well.

The more we reflect the goodness and greatness of God in three Persons, the more we will be likely to serve others in His name. If you're like me, selfless behavior doesn't always come naturally. When I hear Jesus' words "It is more blessed to give than to receive" (Acts 20:35), I usually think, *Can I hear my options first?* I happen to like receiving. I like being waited on. So I'm supposed to live with a servant's heart that models the selfless love of the Trinity? That makes me feel like I'm a sleepy teenager who has just been given a Saturday morning chore.

But Jesus' words are true. When I was serving as a missionary to Ivory Coast, I came down with malaria. Living in a large city with an excellent hospital, I was able to recover quickly. A few weeks later, one of my colleagues, Michel, became seriously ill. The only hospital nearby put four patients in a room and one nurse for everyone on the floor. Michel's needs were taken care of by friends and family. But several weeks of his sickness put a strain on his family. So I volunteered to spend the night at the hospital and let Michel's family members stay in my apartment to get a good night's rest.

As I laid on a blanket in that hospital room, I couldn't help but laugh at the situation I'd gotten myself into. I laughed right up to the point I was told Michel's colostomy bag had to be changed. Of course, I was there to serve, so I did what any good missionary would do—I looked for the nurse! The nurse on duty handed me a pair of gloves and a bedpan and then talked me through the process. When that night was over, I remember thinking that despite the fear and discomfort, there was joy in serving.

Salvation is about partaking of the love and fellowship of the Trinity. The self-giving, outward focus of God's love is the basis for our self-giving, outward focus in mission. That's why we are called to lose our lives in order to gain them (Mark 8:35). It's in giving of ourselves and delighting in God and in others that we reflect His love to the world around us.

VOICES FROM *the Church*

"When something is useful you are attracted to it for what it can bring you or do for you. But if it is beautiful, then you enjoy it simply for what it is. Just being in its presence is its own reward. To glorify someone is also to serve or defer to him or her. Instead of sacrificing their interests to make yourself happy, you sacrifice your interests to make them happy. Why? Your ultimate joy is to see them in joy."[6]
–Timothy Keller

The Father, Son, and Spirit are equally and fully God (1 Pet. 1:1-2).

1 *Peter, an apostle of Jesus Christ:*

To the temporary residents dispersed in Pontus, Galatia, Cappadocia, Asia, and Bithynia, chosen 2 *according to the foreknowledge of God the Father and set apart by the Spirit for obedience and for sprinkling with the blood of Jesus Christ.*
May grace and peace be multiplied to you.

Take a look at the trinitarian elements in the passage we just read. Peter intended to offer words of assurance that would bring comfort to believers facing persecution. His audience was likely made up of Gentile Christians who had left a life of idolatry (4:3), ignorance (1:14), and emptiness (1:18) before they came to Christ. One of his purposes for this letter was to remind these believers that before, they were "not a people," but now they are "God's people" (2:10).

So how does this letter of assurance begin? With a reminder of who believers are and who God is. You see, shallow visions of God do not sustain Christians in the midst of persecution and trial. When we lean on the everlasting arms of God, we need to be reassured that those arms are indeed everlasting. The beauty of the gospel is that God is the One who saves, and all three Persons are involved in this salvation.

Peter mentioned how we are "chosen according to the foreknowledge of God the Father." Salvation starts in the heart of God, and the Bible tells the story of God's redemptive plan to rescue people from sin and death. Peter mentioned how believers are "set apart...for sprinkling with the blood of Jesus Christ." Here we see the Son at work, the One whose blood covers our sin. Peter also mentioned that we are "set apart by the Spirit for obedience." It is the Spirit of holiness who empowers us to live as God's set-apart people.

Make no mistake. The New Testament teaches that the three Persons of the Trinity, who are active in our salvation, are each fully and equally God. Consider how Thomas responded when he beheld the risen Jesus: "My Lord and my God!" (John 20:28)—a shocking affirmation from a Jewish man steeped in the scriptural teaching that "the LORD is One." But Jesus didn't correct Him. Instead, He blessed others who come to the same conclusion.

Likewise, the New Testament speaks of the Holy Spirit with language generally reserved for God. In Paul's First Letter to the Corinthians, we learn that "the Spirit searches everything, even the depths of God." He went on to say, "For who among men knows the thoughts of a man except the spirit of the man that is in him? In the same way, no one knows the thoughts of God except the Spirit of God" (2:10-11).

So what's the takeaway? Yes, the three Persons have diverse roles, but They are a unity. What does this mean for the church? Just this—believers reflect the triune nature of God as we are united by the gospel and diverse in our roles. First, consider the importance of our unity. Paul wrote to the church in Corinth to remind them of their baptism by one Spirit into the body of Christ (1 Cor. 12). The unity of the members is based in God's loving action on their behalf.

At the same time, their unity is demonstrated in their diversity. They are one body but many members. They are all united as part of the family of God, and yet they are diverse in background: Jews and Greeks, slaves and free. They all have the Spirit dwelling in them, and yet they are diverse in their gifts and talents for ministry in the church. Unity and diversity. The Bible ends with a vision of a "vast multitude from every nation, tribe, people, and language, which no one could number, standing before the throne and before the Lamb…And they cried out in a loud voice: Salvation belongs to our God, who is seated on the throne, and to the Lamb!" (Rev. 7:9-10).

The church is a window to a watching world of God's future reign as King of His creation. As God's children, we should celebrate the diversity among us, regardless of our earthly citizenship, social background, or race and ethnicity. But unity in diversity is only possible when we are focused first on the Lord God, who is One in three Persons. When we properly reflect our triune God, we find ourselves ready to love and serve others.

Conclusion

The point of knowing about God is that we come to know God. Theology is not an exercise in head-scratching puzzles but a discipline that should lead to heart-stirring emotions. In this session, we've seen the biblical truth that we serve one God in three Persons. The goal of Christian teaching is love, and love is what we see when we peer into the mystery of the Trinity. Love is the source of our existence, and love sums up the goal of our lives. The triune God made us for Himself. O come, let us adore Him!

Devotions

WHAT GOOD IS IT?

James 2:14-16: "What good is it, my brothers, if someone says he has faith but does not have works? Can his faith save him? If a brother or sister is without clothes and lacks daily food and one of you says to them, 'Go in peace, keep warm, and eat well,' but you don't give them what the body needs, what good is it?"

Over the previous 12 chapters, we have learned a lot about God. Yet it is easy to feel that there is still so much more to learn. In our final chapter, let's ask ourselves, *So what? What differences have the past few chapters made in our lives?*

If you are like me, I will always try to err on the side of less work when possible—especially if it makes it look like I have more faith! But the Bible pushes us to action. Yes, salvation is by grace. According to Ephesians 2:8-9, it is not anything we have done on our own. But the very next verse says that we were created for good works that God has prepared for us (2:10).

Likewise, James warned against the kind of theologizing "faith" that doesn't lead to good works. The doctrine of God is the most important subject we could study. But the purpose for our study is that our hearts would be awed by His splendor and our feet would be moved toward His mission.

Pause and Reflect

1   Take a moment to write out how your faith has been challenged and strengthened over the past few chapters as you have learned more about God.

- -

2   Is there something God has been nudging you to do in response to these studies that you have been resisting? If so, what is something you can do right now to move in the direction of obedience?

SET APART

Romans 12:1: "Therefore, brothers, by the mercies of God, I urge you to present your bodies as a living sacrifice, holy and pleasing to God; this is your spiritual worship."

As a freshman in college, I had only been a follower of Christ for a year. All the insights I received in Bible study were new to me.

One night, our Bible study group was talking about holiness. The leader started off with the idea that every one of us in that room was called to be "holy," or "set apart" for God's service. He used the example of a pair of "set apart" basketball shoes he had in high school. He never wore these shoes except when he was on a basketball court—never out to the car, never on the track, never even at his house. These shoes were "set apart" for one use only—to play basketball.

What seems overly simplistic now was life altering for me then. I didn't know much, but I could understand this—I was set apart. As a new believer, I came to realize my purpose. I knew at that time what I was supposed to be focused on.

At one time, I had been focused on things that are opposed to God. But not anymore. I was reconciled to Christ through His death, and it was on the basis of His work for me that I could be presented to God as "holy, faultless, and blameless before Him." Christ presents us as blameless based on what He accomplished on the cross. Our task is simply to stay grounded and steadfast in the faith, not losing hope in the good news of this gospel (Col. 1:21-23).

Pause and Reflect

1   What seemingly mundane or simple thing in your life have you set apart for a very specific purpose? What are the benefits of doing so?

---

2   Read 1 Peter 1:14-19, and consider why God has the authority to set us apart for Himself.

---

3   How can being set apart often be difficult and also wonderful (Heb. 12:10-13)?

So the World May Believe

John 17:21: "May they all be one, as You, Father, are in Me and I am in You. May they also be one in Us, so the world may believe You sent Me."

In John 17, Jesus begins praying for Himself (vv. 1-5), for His disciples (vv. 6-19), and then finally for future believers (vv. 20-26). Jesus prayed for us. He prayed that we would be unified and loving so the world would believe God sent Jesus. Jesus prayed that we would be as unified as He and the Father are.

Jesus concluded with these words: "Righteous Father! The world has not known You. However, I have known You, and these have known that You sent Me. I made Your name known to them and will make it known, so the love You have loved Me with may be in them and I may be in them" (vv. 25-26).

This unity Jesus prayed for is possible only because of the unity of the triune God (John 14:10-11; 15:4-5). It is possible for your church to be unified. Jesus said so, and He prayed for it. It didn't take that long to begin to see it happening. In Acts 2, we see the first evidence of this with the sending of the Spirit and God gathering people from many nations and tongues (Acts 2:14-42).

Pause and Reflect

1   Read Acts 2:41-47. Think about how this first church spent their time. What seems feasible in our churches today, and what seems impossible?

- -

2   How does the unity of God in three Persons affect your view of church unity?

DISCUSSION QUESTIONS

1   The word *Trinity* does not appear in Scripture. How then do we discover biblical teaching on this topic? In what ways does using a word like this aid our understanding?

2   Read James 2:14-26. Who else believes that God is one? Describe the difference in believing this truth as a fact and living it out with devotion.

3   What are some common things and relationships that rival God for our devotion? How does the truth of God's oneness relate to the truth that we should have an undivided heart for the Lord?

4   What encouragement do you find in the complexity of the Bible's teaching about God? What challenges? Do you find your faith strengthened or challenged by these truths?

5   When you hear the command to love your neighbor as yourself, are you tempted to picture yourself doing miserable chores with no reward other than fulfilling an obligation? How does that conflict with the picture of how the three Persons of the Trinity relate to one another?

6   Think of a time when you experienced joy in service. Did you have to overcome a sense of reluctance? Was there a change in how you thought about serving others afterward?

7   How would your life be different if two or three of your most significant relationships were increasingly more others-centered rather than self-centered in focus? How hopeful are you that this is possible?

8   In what ways does the truth that all three Persons of the Trinity were actively involved in our salvation increase our awe and wonder at the beauty of the gospel?

9   In what ways can your church celebrate unity of purpose and diversity of gifts and personalities? How can our churches better represent God's triune nature by pursuing diversity? How closely does your church reflect the diversity of the community where it is located? How comfortable would people of a different cultural or racial background be if they visited your church?

Endnotes

Chapter 1

1. A. W. Tozer, *The Knowledge of the Holy* (New York: HarperCollins, 1961), 1.
2. Henry T. Blackaby and Richard Blackaby, *Experiencing God Day-by-Day* (Nashville: Broadman & Holman Publishers, 1998), 12.
3. Tim Keller, "The Gospel and the Supremacy of Christ in a Postmodern World," in *The Supremacy of Christ in a Postmodern World*, gen. eds. John Piper and Justin Taylor (Wheaton: Crossway, 2007), 111-12.
4. J. I. Packer, *Knowing God* (Downers Grove: InterVarsity Press, 1973), 23.
5. C. S. Lewis, *Reflections on the Psalms* (New York: Harcourt, Brace and Company, 1958), 93-95.
6. Irenaeus, *Irenaeus Against Heresies*, in *Ante-Nicene Fathers*, eds. Alexander Roberts, James Donaldson, and A. Cleveland Coxe, vol. 1 (Peabody, MA: Hendrickson, 1885), 469.

Chapter 2

1. C. S. Lewis, *Mere Christianity* (New York: Touchstone, 1980), 45-46.
2. Ben Patterson, *God's Prayer Book* (Carol Stream, IL: Tyndale, 2008), 56.
3. Alister E. McGrath, *Christian Theology: An Introduction*, 4th ed. (Malden, MA: Blackwell Publishing, 2007), 190-92.
4. Ibid., 388.
5. William Lane Craig, "The Existence of God and the Beginning of the Universe," *Truth Journal*, Leadership U [online; cited 26 October 2012]. Available from the Internet: *www.leaderu.com*.
6. William Lane Craig, "Moral Argument," Reasonable Faith [online; cited 29 October 2012]. Available from the Internet: *www.reasonablefaith.org*.
7. Jeff Schreve, "Practical Atheism?" Crosswalk.com [online], 5 March [cited 29 October 2012]. Available from the Internet: *www.crosswalk.com*.
8. John of Damascus, "Treatise II," in *Three Treatises on the Divine Images* (Crestwood, NY: St. Vladimir's Seminary Press, 2003), 70-71.

Chapter 3

1. John Stott, *The Contemporary Christian* (Downers Grove: InterVarsity Press, 1992), 39.
2. Mark Galli, *A Great and Terrible Love* (Grand Rapids: Baker Books, 2009), 69.
3. Anselm of Canterbury, *Proslogion*, quoted in *Christian Theology: An Introduction*, by Alister E. McGrath, 4th ed., 34.

Chapter 4

1. J. I. Packer, *Knowing God*, 83.
2. Ben Patterson, *God's Prayer Book*, 294.

Chapter 5

1. Menno Simons, "A Meditation on the Twenty-fifth Psalm," in *Early Anabaptist Spirituality: Selected Writings*, trans. and ed. Daniel Liechty (Mahwah, NJ: Paulist Press, 1994), 251.
2. Francis Chan and Danae Yankoski, *Crazy Love* (Colorado Springs: David C. Cook, 2008), 59.
3. Wayne Grudem, *Systematic Theology* (Grand Rapids: Zondervan, 1994), 197.
4. C. S. Lewis, *The Four Loves* (New York: Harcourt, Inc., 1988).
5. Robert W. Yarbrough, *ESV Study Bible* (Wheaton: Crossway Bibles, 2008), 2431, n. 2:2.

Chapter 6

1. Adrian Rogers, *Adrianisms: The Wit and Wisdom of Adrian Rogers*, vol. 2 (Memphis: Love Worth Finding Ministries, 2007), 3.
2. Trevin Wax, *Counterfeit Gospels* (Chicago: Moody Press, 2011), 77.
3. Wayne Grudem, *Systematic Theology*, 202.
4. Millard J. Erickson, *Christian Theology*, 2nd ed. (Grand Rapids: Baker Books, 1998), 313-15.
5. Wayne Grudem, *Systematic Theology*, 206.
6. Ibid., 205.
7. Wayne Martindale and Jerry Root, *The Quotable Lewis* (Carol Stream, IL: Tyndale, 1989), 249.
8. Francis Dubose, "Love: The Mood and Method of Mission," in *The Mission of God Study Bible*, eds. Ed Stetzer and Philip Nation (Nashville: Holman Bible Publishers, 2012), 1124.

Chapter 7

1. Sam Storms, *The Hope of Glory* (Wheaton: Crossway, 2008), 95.
2. C. S. Lewis, *Mere Christianity*, 56.

Chapter 8

1. Augustine, "Sermon 9: Christmas," in *St. Augustine: Sermons for Christmas and Epiphany*, vol. 15 in *Ancient Christian Writers: The Works of the Fathers in Translation*, eds. Johannes Quasten and Joseph C. Plumpe (New York: Paulist Press, 1952) 107.
2. Herschel H. Hobbs, *The Baptist Faith and Message*, rev. ed. (Nashville: Convention Press, 1971), 39.
3. Marva Dawn, *Talking the Walk* (Grand Rapids: Brazos Press, 2005), 40.
4. J. I. Packer, *Knowing God*, 53.

Chapter 9

1. John Wesley, "A Letter to a Roman Catholic," in *The Works of the Rev. John Wesley*, vol. IX (New York: J. & J. Harper, 1827), 532.
2. Chrysostom, *Homilies on the Epistle to the Hebrews*, in *Nicene and Post-Nicene Fathers, First Series*, ed. Philip Schaff, vol. 14 (Peabody, MA: Hendrickson Publishers, 1889), 389.

Chapter 10

1. Augustine, *Lectures or Tractates on the Gospel According to St. John*, 74:1, in *Nicene and Post-Nicene Fathers, First Series*, ed. Philip Schaff, vol. 7 (Peabody, MA: Hendrickson Publishers, 1888), 333.
2. Francis Chan and Danae Yankoski, *Forgotten God: Reversing Our Tragic Neglect of the Holy Spirit* (Colorado Springs: David C. Cook, 2009), 18.
3. Sinclair B. Ferguson, *The Holy Spirit*, in *Contours of Christian Theology*, gen. ed. Gerald Bray (Downers Grove: InterVarsity Press, 1996), 71.
4. Francis Chan and Danae Yankoski, *Forgotten God: Reversing Our Tragic Neglect of the Holy Spirit*, 34-35.
5. Arthur Bennett, ed., *The Valley of Vision* (Carlisle, PA: The Banner of Truth Trust, 1975), 29.
6. Wayne Grudem, *Systematic Theology*, 195.
7. Francis Chan and Danae Yankoski, *Forgotten God: Reversing Our Tragic Neglect of the Holy Spirit*, 76.

Chapter 11

1. J. I. Packer, *Keep in Step with the Spirit*, 2nd ed. (Grand Rapids: Baker Books, 2005), 15.
2. D. L. Moody, *The D. L. Moody Yearbook*, in *The D. L. Moody Collection*, ed. and comp. James S. Bell Jr. (Chicago: Moody Press, 1997), 367.
3. Michael Kelley, *Holy Vocabulary* (Nashville: LifeWay Press, 2010), 90.

Chapter 12

1. Robertson McQuilkin, quoted in *Transformational Discipleship*, by Eric Geiger, Michael Kelley, and Philip Nation (Nashville: B&H Publishing Group, 2011), 222.
2. Thomas Watson, *A Body of Divinity, Contained in Sermons upon the Assembly's Catechism*, rev. by George Rogers (London: Passmore & Alabaster, 1881), 159.
3. Wayne Grudem, *Systematic Theology*, 1016.
4. Michael Kelley, *Holy Vocabulary*, 93-94.

Chapter 13

1. Josh Harris, *Dug Down Deep* (Colorado Springs: Multnomah, 2010), 51.
2. Francis A. Schaeffer, *True Spirituality*, in *A Christian View of Spirituality*, vol. 3 in *The Complete Works of Francis A. Schaeffer: A Christian Worldview* (Wheaton: Crossway Books, 1982), 271.
3. Augustine, *On the Trinity*, 1.3.5, in *Nicene and Post-Nicene Fathers, First Series*, ed. Philip Schaff, vol. 3 (Peabody, MA: Hendrickson Publishers, 1887), 19.
4. B. B. Warfield, *Biblical Foundations* (London: The Tyndale Press, 1958), 79, quoted in *He Who Gives Life: The Doctrine of the Holy Spirit*, by Graham A. Cole (Wheaton: Crossway Books, 2007), 64.
5. Bruce A. Ware, *Father, Son, and Holy Spirit: Relationships, Roles, and Relevance* (Wheaton: Crossway Books, 2005), 20.
6. Timothy Keller, *The Reason for God* (New York: Dutton, 2008), 214.

How to Use This Resource

Welcome to *The Gospel Project*, a gospel-centered curriculum that dives deep into the things of God, lifts up Jesus, focuses on the grand story of Scripture, and drives participants to be on mission. This short-term resource provides opportunities to study the Bible and to encounter the living Christ. *The Gospel Project* provides you with tools and resources to purposefully study God's Word and to grow in the faith and knowledge of God's Son. And what's more, you can do so in the company of others, encouraging and building up one another.

Here are some things to remember that will help you maximize the usefulness of this resource:

Gather a Group. We grow in the faith best in community with other believers, as we love, encourage, correct, and challenge one another. The life of a disciple of Christ was never meant to be lived alone, in isolation.

Pray. Pray regularly for your group members.

Prepare. This resource includes the Bible study content, three devotionals, and follow-up questions for each chapter. Work through the chapter and devotionals in preparation for each group session. Take notes and record your own questions. Also consider the follow-up questions so you are ready to participate in and add to the discussion, bringing up your own notes and questions where appropriate.

Resource Yourself. Make good use of the additional resources available on the Web at *www.gospelproject.com/additionalresources*. Download a podcast. Read a blog post. Be intentional about learning from others in the faith.

Group Time. Gather together with your group to discuss the chapter and devotional content. Work through the follow-up questions and your own questions. Discuss the material and the implications for the lives of believers and the mission to which we have been called.

Overflow. Remember...*The Gospel Project* is not just a curriculum. WE are the project. The gospel is working on us. Don't let your preparation time be simply about the content. Let the truths of God's Word soak in as you study. Let God work on your heart first, and then pray that He will change the hearts of the other people in your group.

Small Group Tips

Reading through this section and utilizing the suggested principles and practices will greatly enhance the group experience. First is to accept your limitations. You cannot transform a life. Your group must be devoted to the Bible, the Holy Spirit, and the power of Christian community. In doing so your group will have all the tools necessary to draw closer to God and to each other—and to experience heart transformation.

General Tips

• Prepare for each meeting by reviewing the material, praying for each group member, and asking the Holy Spirit to work through you as you point to Jesus each week.

• Make new attendees feel welcome.

• Think of ways to connect with group members away from group time. The amount of participation you have during your group meetings is directly related to the amount of time you connect with your group members away from the group meeting. Consider sending e-mails, texts, or social networking messages encouraging members in their personal devotion times prior to the session.

Materials Needed

• Bible

• Bible study book

• Pen/pencil

Provide Resources for Guests

An inexpensive way to make first-time guests feel welcome is to provide them a copy of your Bible study book. Estimate how many first-time guests you can expect during the course of your study, and secure that number of books. What about people who have not yet visited your group? You can encourage them to visit by providing a copy of the Bible study book.

Let People Tell Their Stories

If people in the group seem to be shy or have trouble participating in discussion, ask the group for a personal example of something that relates to the larger point and then use that personal experience to springboard into a larger discussion:

• "What is one time on a vacation when your plans didn't go exactly right?" (for moving into a discussion of patience).

• "Tell us about a time when your children did something that genuinely made you happy" (for moving into a discussion about obedience and love).

Using these stories fosters the kind of open atmosphere you're looking for and at the same time makes people more willing and confident in contributing.

Michael Kelley, "Five Things Every Group Leader Should Do," 9Marks Journal [online], January/February 2012 [cited 13 December 2012]. Available from the Internet: *www.9marks.org.*

Encourage Your Group Members to Get a GRIP

Each Christian is uniquely designed by God to contribute to his or her small group. Four areas in particular provide opportunities for a person to lovingly give of themselves for the sake of the others: **G-R-I-P.**

• Spiritual **G**ifts. These are given to believers by the Holy Spirit to be exercised in His power for the benefit of others. We have been given different gifts in order to highlight our need for unity.

• **R**esources. Our individual skills, abilities, possessions, and time are to be put to use for the blessing of others.

• **I**ndividual experiences. The unique experiences and past of group members serve to display the variety of God's work in His people.

• **P**assions. One member's passion for a ministry or calling can encourage others to participate and even ignite their own passions for God's work.

Rick Howerton, *Destination: Community* (Nashville: Serendipity House, 2007), 107-12.

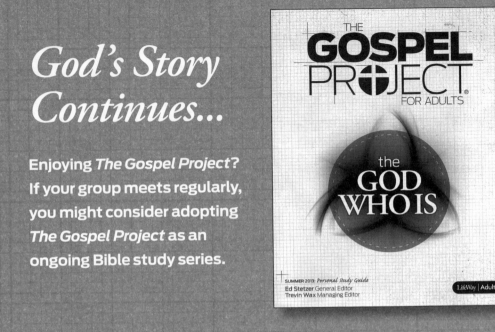

God's Story Continues...

Enjoying *The Gospel Project*? If your group meets regularly, you might consider adopting *The Gospel Project* as an ongoing Bible study series.

THE **GOSPEL PROJECT** FOR ADULTS®

the **GOD WHO IS**

SUMMER 2013: *Personal Study Guide*
Ed Stetzer General Editor
Trevin Wax Managing Editor

LifeWay | Adults

Reasons to switch to ongoing studies

Consistency: The ongoing format helps ensure that you will be fully established in a gospel-centered understanding of the entire Bible. As you move through *The Gospel Project*, you can rest assured that you are receiving robust biblical teaching all year long.

Community: When you join thousands of other groups working through the same topics at the same time, you receive the benefit of online interaction through *The Gospel Project* blog.

Cost: Jumping in with our ongoing format is the most affordable option over time.

The Gospel Project is available for kids, students, and adults so that your entire church family can explore the grand narrative of redemption history together. Available in print and digital formats, it is easy to choose the option that works best for you. For more information on *The Gospel Project* and to order, visit *gospelproject.com*.

Web: **gospelproject.com** Twitter: **@Gospel_Project** Facebook: **TheGospelProject**